Dedication

From Libby
This book is dedicated to my parents, Parks and Sarah Pedrick, who, despite all the zany, hair-brained, and wild ideas I pursued, made sure that I was instilled with a strong foundation of core values and personal beliefs.

From Martha
For Alan Downs, Melanie "Miel" Keveles, and Judi Neal—for everything that matters more than anything.

HR from the Heart

Inspiring Stories and Strategies for Building
the People Side of Great Business

Libby Sartain
with
Martha I. Finney

AMACOM
American Management Association
New York • Atlanta • Brussels • Buenos Aires • Chicago • London • Mexico City
San Francisco • Shanghai • Tokyo • Toronto • Washington, D. C.

Special discounts on bulk quantities of AMACOM books are available to corporations, professional associations, and other organizations. For details, contact Special Sales Department, AMACOM, a division of American Management Association, 1601 Broadway, New York, NY 10019.
Tel.: 212-903-8316   Fax: 212-903-8083
Web site: www.amacombooks.org

This publication is designed to provide accurate and authoritative information in regard to the subject matter covered. It is sold with the understanding that the publisher is not engaged in rendering legal, accounting, or other professional service. If legal advice or other expert assistance is required, the services of a competent professional person should be sought.

Library of Congress Cataloging-in-Publication Data

Sartain, Libby, 1954-
  HR from the heart : inspiring stories and strategies for building the
people side of great business / Libby Sartain with Martha I. Finney.
      p. cm.
Includes bibliographical references and index.
  ISBN 0-8144-0756-0
  1. Personnel management. 2. Personnel departments—Management.
3. Personnel management—Vocational guidance. 4. Customer relations.
5. Industrial relations. I. Finney, Martha I. II. Title.

HF5549 .S1753 2003
658.3—dc21   2002152889

Printing number
10 9 8

Contents

PART 2:
HR Is Your Company's Best Asset

Contents

Foreword

Have you ever wondered what the world would it be like if we could read people's minds? And if we could, how would that ability affect the human resources (HR) profession? One thing is certain, we would do away with much of the uncertainty we experience in workplace relationships. And we could even quantify and evaluate the HR processes and functions that previously eluded measurement, enhancing our efforts to perform at a high level, and helping others in the organization improve their work as well.

Sounds like science fiction, right? Not really. There is a brave new world of knowledge to which most of us pay little attention and few have been able to measure. It is a body of knowledge that is as complex as the individuals who seek to obtain it.

Introspection. Self-awareness. Knowledge of ourselves.

Reading our own minds goes beyond acknowledging the basic information required to be a competent employee, manager, or HR professional. It is discovering the heart of who we are—our character, personality, ethics, and the ability to relate to others. Think about how important such knowledge is in organizations of all kinds, and its special relevance to those of us in HR as we seek to attract and retain talented employees and develop and deliver policies and programs that improve workplace efficiency, creativity, and productivity. The more we know about ourselves—the more we can get into our own minds—the better able we are to assist the diverse workforce we serve.

Ancient philosophers understood that. The Greek thinker and teacher Socrates believed that the search for knowledge began with introspection: "Know thyself." He taught his students that they should question themselves about various things in life. By following each question with another question, the person would eventually realize that they had the final answer within themselves—or, in some cases, that there was no final answer to be found. Psychologists say it is comparable to peeling an onion, discovering new complex behaviors as each layer is revealed. The process is called the Socratic Dialogue or Method, and it is still used among students of philosophy and law today.

But it is Greek to most of us. We either do not know it exists or, if we do, we hardly ever use it due to the time constraints of competing responsibilities. We as HR professionals focus on other people in the organization without first establishing the basic foundation for understanding—knowledge of self.

Maybe that is why people are generally unaware of how they interact with others in given situations. We do not spend enough time evaluating how our personal values, feelings, strengths, and weaknesses affect our relationships and responsibilities in and outside of the workplace. As managers, not understanding what makes us tick can stifle our development because we are using less than 100% of our internal resources. That can hurt our chances for achieving great success in the workplace.

Some researchers have classified this search for self-knowledge as "Emotional Intelligence (EI)." Studies indicate (and quantify) just how important it is: top performance is based on 80 percent EI compared with 20 percent for IQ. Adherents say that it can be taught. As a result, measurement instruments are being developed and utilized. Some organizations are even implementing EI strategies within their workforces. But the entire concept is still dependent on an individual's desire to pursue self-knowledge.

For HR professionals today, it is not enough that they focus on acquiring self-knowledge for the sake of feeling good about themselves. Acquiring a keen sense of self is dependent on HR professionals becoming adept at reading the minds of their CEOs—knowing, understanding and speaking the language of business. And for good reason.

A number of strategic trends in the current business environment—the increasing value of human capital in the marketplace, globalization of U.S. companies, and the emergence of technologies that have changed (and continue to change) the fundamentals for how employees and their companies interact—have created a new set of opportunities and challenges for the HR profession.

These opportunities and challenges demand that HR professionals demonstrate mastery in both the technical and "human" HR competencies that set them apart as guardians of human capital management. It is the seamless integration of these skill sets—emotional intelligence combined with business acumen—that makes a successful HR leader; one who can translate who they are and what they know into tangible contributions that positively impact their organization's bottom line.

It is this integration that is depicted in Libby Sartain's book. And it is this understanding of mind and heart, business know-how, and from-the-heart passion, to which she challenges all of us to aspire.

Are we up for the challenge of discovering the mysteries contained in our own minds? If it means that we will acquire the skill set required to evaluate the HR functions that have previously eluded measurement, count me in. We have to start somewhere. For now, starting the process is as simple as asking oneself a question.

Susan R. Meisinger, SPHR
President and Chief Executive Officer
Society for Human Resource Management

Acknowledgments

I am always amazed by the seemingly random way in which simple decisions and circumstances can alter the course of our lives. Job choices, new bosses, even a chance encounter with a stranger may become the basis of future long-term relationships with talented and wise people whose influence, support, mentoring, and friendship shape our values and beliefs, form our communication styles, add to our knowledge base, challenge our thinking, and make us who we are. Without such blessings, my career experiences and the knowledge upon which this book is based would never have come about. Even among old friends, a spark of inspiration, a casual remark, or a suggestion can send us to surprising new destinations. At the moment, I'm thinking specifically of a "good-bye" lunch that was held for me as I was preparing to leave Southwest Airlines after thirteen years. A long-time business friend, Harry Spring, persuaded me to tackle this project. He said that if I didn't write down exactly what I thought had created the winning people formula at Southwest Airlines, no one would know what had worked so well during the years I was there. My successors would add to and subtract from what we did. It might be better or worse, but it would never be the same. He said that it would be a gift to the HR profession if I shared what I had learned. He also warned me that if I didn't document what I had learned, few would benefit from it. So I have Harry to thank first for being the one to instigate this whole project.

I met my writing partner, Martha Finney, in another pivotal moment—although I didn't realize it at the time. I had just delivered my "Hiring From the Heart" presentation to the Society for Human Resource Management (SHRM) conference in Atlanta in 1999 when she emerged from the audience and handed me her card. A business journalist with an extensive background in writing about HR, she was doing some empirical research into employee engagement and wanted to introduce herself. But life goes on, and we were on separate tracks, making separate decisions that would change our lives separately, although we kept in touch from time to time. Then one coincidental decision ultimately brought us back together: the decision to move to northern California—I from Dallas, and she from Annapolis. So there we were, both living in northern California, at the moment in time when I decided to follow Harry's advice and write a book. Martha added the tremendous value of her understanding of HR, her experience in book publishing, and her wonderful writing style, which will be obvious to the reader. I will be eternally grateful to Martha not only for collaborating with me on the project, but also for sharing her knowledge, teaching me the ropes, and making the arrangements with AMACOM to publish the book, thus leading the way to our editor, Adrienne Hickey. And thanks to Adrienne for being one of those skeptics who are good to have around because they keep you on your toes.

I am extremely thankful for so many people who have affected my career in a significant way. A classmate at Southern Methodist University, Jim Symington, introduced me to a course on organizational behavior that set me in pursuit of an HR career. Mick McGill, Fred Crandall, Jim Tarter, Elvis Stephens, and Frank Rachel were five of the many professors in undergraduate and graduate B-school studies who encouraged my development and my learning of the field. The companies I worked for (National Sharedata Corporation, Mary Kay Cosmetics, Inc., Recognition International, Southwest Airlines, Inc., and Yahoo! Inc.) gave me opportunities to learn and grow and work on innovative initiatives on behalf of our people, as did various leaders with whom I have worked. Thanks in particular to Linda Noble, Judy Stubbs, the late Mary Kay Ash, Manual Guzman, Bill Moore, Mike Kelly, Marcy Lawless, Ann Rhoades, Colleen Barrett, Herb Kelleher, Sue Decker, and Jerry Yang. Many of my coworkers shared their expertise, collaborated on energizing work products, lent creative ideas, and served as a sounding board. I am especially grateful to Ralph Kimmich, Rita Bailey, Sherry Phelps, Lorraine Grubbs West, Alice Larson, Ed Rankin, Linda Drake, Jeff Sullivan, Kathy Rickard, Camille Keith, Ginger Hardage, Beverly Carmichael, Debby Ackerman, Phyllis Adams, Uzma Khan, Laura Sanner, Patti Fleming, Chris Castro, Dan Rosensweig, and Tim Sanders.

SHRM, and its predecessor American Society for Personnel Administration, played as strong a part in my professional life as the positions I held. I first became associated with this organization as a student member, and I have been involved with it for more than twenty-five years. SHRM provided many educational opportunities where I could enhance my knowledge, spot emerging trends, have access to thought leaders, and contribute my knowledge and thoughts to others. Through SHRM, I had a network of fellow HR students, chapter members, and national volunteer leaders, each of whom has made me who I am in some small way, but I am especially grateful to my *Hole-in-the-Wall Gang,* who often kept me sane and always made sure that I had at least one great belly laugh a month. Thanks to the following SHRM members and staff: Kim Sledge Watson, Larry Burk, Karen Bray, Jim Wilkins, Mary Cheddie, Gary Kushner, Melinda Watkins, Gail Parker Aldrich, Neal Bondy, Mike Rogers, Chuck Nielson, Kathy Compton, Sue Meisinger, and Mike Losey.

I would also like to thank a handful of consulting partners with whom I have collaborated on initiatives that led to best practices: Megan Crossin, Mark Schumann, Kevin McDermott, Norman Schippers, Gary Mitchner, and Jim Citrin. Denis Simon, John Spera, and Sam Del Brocco coached me professionally, helping me navigate my way through my own professional and career challenges and helping me find effective ways to communicate my personal brand. Working with experts who were willing to share and transfer knowledge helped me contribute in the best, most innovative ways.

And, most important, I would like to thank my husband and my daughter, who have been there for me all along the way. I met David Sartain more than twenty-five years ago when I tried to recruit him to join the student ASPA chapter at University of North Texas. Since that moment, not only has he supported my career, but he has pushed me further and challenged me to never become stagnant. He has always believed that I would achieve my career goals, and he was there to celebrate every success and to pick up the pieces when things didn't work out as planned. When opportunity knocked for me in Silicon

Valley, he moved halfway across the country and arranged to telecommute so that I could embark on a challenging new career. Anyone who has ever met me knows that my daughter Sarah has been a constant source of pride and joy. She gave my life the meaning and purpose that drove me to achieve at higher levels so that we could provide for her to the best of our abilities and so that I could, I hope, be a model of professional and personal excellence for her in the future. While she had many benefits from a dual-career family, she also endured many hardships because her Mom wasn't always there when she needed me. Thankfully, she waited patiently for me to get home so that we could have many wonderful mother-daughter talks. Thanks to both of you for your love, encouragement, and understanding.

Introduction

Don't get me wrong. I'm not interested in bragging, or in even blowing my own horn. But somewhere along the line people started thinking of me as an HR leader who has the answers. It may be because I've had the marvelous good fortune of working for companies, like Southwest Airlines, Yahoo!, and Mary Kay Cosmetics, that are known as much for being great places to work as they are for the excellence of their products and services. In fact, it is the enthusiasm of their employees that gives these companies the stature they have in their industries. Over the years, many consultants and academics have come into the companies where I've worked to try to capture, graph, and quantify that certain something special that makes these organizations thrive and surpass their own industry standards. They come away with fancy formulas, all of which really boil down to one principle: Companies thrive when (1) they have a high-quality product or service that is needed by their customers, and (2) they are staffed by qualified employees who are dedicated to the corporate mission and who are basically nice, trustworthy, and respectful to one another.

On the flip side, in the more than twenty-five years that I've been in human resources, I've watched the HR profession itself struggle to claim its rightful place among the corporate power players. There seems to be a universal agreement (which I don't necessarily share, at least not all the time) that HR is suffering from low self-esteem as a result of years of criticism by certain business leaders who question the value of our profession. A few highly visible companies have taken to placing non-HR professionals in top HR leadership positions. Consultants around the world are intimidating perfectly well-grounded practitioners with fancy theories and jargon. In the meantime, there are thousands of HR practitioners who are looking for simple, no-pretense ways to bring the best of their own enthusiasm for the field and their professionalism to the corporate world, so that they can invest their own talents and drive to grow their companies, the careers of their co-workers, and their own careers as far as they want to go.

If you are a member of this group, this book is for you. My goal for *HR From the Heart* is to share the message that smart and talented human resource professionals can build a rewarding career that is consistent with their personal values and beliefs—*and* can use their business smarts to grow exciting companies by harnessing the talents, passions, and smarts of their people. It is a matter of bringing the best of your most authentic self into your professional life and finding ways to help the employees of your organization do the same. That is the simple path to growing a thriving company with fully engaged employees.

Not Just Another Southwest Kiss-and-Tell

Although I am now at Yahoo!, I am still best known for my thirteen years at Southwest Airlines. And I imagine several people will pick up this book looking for the inside scoop on a company and its leaders that I have admired and loved over the years. Others might be tempted to dismiss this book as yet another product of a Southwest employee trying to cash in on Southwest's spirit and fame. It wouldn't surprise me if they did; I've seen enough of those gimmicks to last a lifetime. As my writing partner, Martha Finney, and I worked hard over the last year to gather and express the best wisdom, advice, and observations from all my years in HR, I've been burdened with my own personal anxiety that *HR From the Heart* will be associated with the many fly-by-night employees who worked at Southwest for only a very short time, with the sole objective of capitalizing on their ever-so-brief experience on the "inside" by taking their show on the road and making their fortunes by spouting their versions of Southwest wisdom.

On the contrary, I have been approached by publishers many times over the years with suggestions that I write a book about Southwest and tell how "I created the *HR legend*." I didn't create Southwest Airlines, and I certainly didn't create the HR legend. While I was at Southwest, I was a member of several teams—a visionary senior leadership team and a team of some of the best HR people that I know. Our results weren't always glowing. Sometimes our efforts worked, and sometimes we flubbed it. But all my experiences inside Southwest had more of an influence on me than I had on the people function or the company as a whole.

Yes, most of the stories in this book are taken from my experiences at Southwest, primarily because that's where I have spent the bulk of my career so far. They're stories that I am proud to share—not because I was the hero of them, but because all the wonderful people around me were the heroes. What I've been teaching in recent years is what I've learned from the heartening examples, the courage, the vision, the selflessness, and the enthusiasm of all the people with whom I've had the privilege to be associated over a quarter century. And it is my additional privilege to pass these lessons on to you and make them a permanent part of the HR body of knowledge.

Why This Book Is Different

First of all, books about the HR profession that were written by HR practitioners are rare. The books you'll find on HR are about the theory and practice of HR functions, and they were written by consultants and academics. *HR From the Heart* is the first book *by* an HR practitioner *for* HR practitioners about managing your own unique career as well as dealing with the special challenges of daily life in the world of human resources.

This is the first book on HR that has the nerve to be up-front and center with the word *heart*. The fundamental principle of this book—and of my entire career, for that matter—is that in human resources, *head* and *heart* should not be considered mutually exclusive. Over the last couple of decades, we've been so distracted by the need to be taken seriously that we've been tempted to jettison any discussion of how our personal feelings and principles are factored into the business equation. As a result, the HR profession has been cultivating a reputation that I'm tempted to say it often deserves—that of being a single-minded administrator with a big, red, rubber stamp that reads: "No! Against Policy and Procedures!"

In the introduction to most business books, at this point there would be a quick outline of all the chapters and their main points (for those busy, extroverted business leaders who really don't have the time to sit down and read the book but would like to appear to be conversant with its contents at cocktail parties and in conference hospitality suites). Because this book has forty-four chapters, I'm going to spare you. But I would like to take this opportunity to outline the basic principles upon which this entire book is written:

- The fully empowered HR career is a calling.

- The fully empowered HR function is a competitive advantage.

- For HR to make the impact it needs to make, you have to be a businessperson first.

- A corporate culture that is based on respectful treatment of all the company's employees is essential to the company's long-term success.

- The most successful companies are the ones that make it their business to help their employees achieve their highest potential and use their gifts and talents most fully.

- It is a waste of your time to settle for anything less.

You and I both know that in its heart of hearts, the human resource profession is full of creative promise. This is where the company's *best assets* begin their relationship with their employer. And this is where the lives and futures of millions of people and their families all over the world take shape. This is where we have a tremendous capacity to make an incredible difference in corporate health, economic health, and the quality of life for everyone who says yes to the job offers we extend.

This book is not an authoritarian set of instructions on what and how to think about the way you manage HR within your company. It's a friendly invitation to spend some time with me to explore a fresh look at how we can combine the best of our strategic abilities in the corporate setting, our content expertise, and our enthusiasm for the human adventure to create incredible careers for ourselves in human resource management and build great businesses.

PART 1

Your Own Career Is Your Best HR Asset

CHAPTER 1

What's Love Got to Do with It?

This is a book about love. And it's a book about strategy. And it's about motivation. And profit. And politics. And courage. And mission. And competition. And kindness. And discipline. And speaking out. And staying quiet. It's about using your head and working from the heart. This is a book about human resource management.

But this book is about more than just the theory and practice of human resource management. It's also about growing your own career in HR, starting from wherever you are and going all the way to that proverbial "seat at the table," if that's where you ultimately want to go. This book is about helping you cultivate a career that you love.

I suppose I've always been about love and work. The fact that for thirteen years I was associated with Southwest Airlines (the "love" airline, headquartered at Love Field in Dallas) is strictly coincidental. The fact that I'm known among my peers and colleagues as the poster person for promoting this profession that I love . . . well, that's not a coincidence. I wouldn't have it any other way. And neither should you.

I'd like to start this book by saying right here and now that I'm passionate about HR. In fact, I'll even go so far as to say exactly what it is to me: a calling. If you're not especially religious, the idea of a calling may be unsettling—especially the idea of a corporate leader discussing it in a mainstream business book like this one. Don't worry, this isn't going to be a religious book. But it is going to be an invitation to you to put the HR profession on a more elevated platform.

Yes, it's true: The daily details remain. As an HR practitioner, you are still responsible for compliance and administrative details. How well you acquire and manage the talent pool can make the difference between a successful new initiative and a failure. Yes, it's true that much of what you do can be boiled down into metrics, outcomes, spreadsheets, equations, formulas, and profit and loss. However, HR is also a huge—some would say *sacred*—responsibility because as an HR leader you are entrusted with other people's futures, needs, and work-life well-being. All those deliverables and decisions that you have a hand in developing directly influence not only the financial viability of your company but also the private life of each and every individual who is associated with your business—your employees; your leaders; your vendors, suppliers, and consultants; even your customers. With this kind of responsibility, you must approach your profession with both competency and passion.

I get frustrated when I meet HR practitioners who don't see that vision—who don't see the connection that HR professionals can create between their individual passion and organizational strategy. There are probably more of those practitioners than we'd like to admit. I know for a fact that there are far too many HR practitioners who fell into the profession with no real understanding or appreciation of the profound responsibility and the amazing privilege of this career. They're there because they think HR will give them the power to be a policy maker or a power broker. And then there are other HR practitioners who pride themselves on being *people* people. They want to be corporate cruise directors, making everyone happy, and they have no real understanding of the fact that they are working within a business and that what they do must succeed, fulfill the needs of the for-profit organization, and further corporate objectives.

I also know for a fact that there are many more HR professionals who absolutely recognize the amazing gift of their HR careers. But they are shy about expressing their passion, for fear of losing their professional image as clear-eyed, clear-thinking businesspeople. But privately, they know that the two perspectives of HR aren't mutually exclusive. On the contrary, these two perspectives are mutually dependent if you are to be successful and to be part of an amazingly successful business that defies all odds—a company like Southwest Airlines, for instance.

That kind of melding of perspectives depends on the emotional, intellectual, and strategic strength of HR professionals who have the courage to invest both their heart and their smarts in what they do. When they do this, all of the other issues affecting the HR role in business fall into place.

I invite you to take a serious look at your role in HR. How does that role add value to your company's business? How does that role support and nurture the careers of the people who work for your company? What can you do to create a workplace community that allows business to get done, and in which the individuals who work at your company can invest their talents, skills, and passion daily and, in turn, feel inspired and engaged by the opportunities your company offers?

This is the calling of HR. And this is the opportunity. And never before has it been so exciting and compelling.

And this is my invitation to you: to take a fresh look at our profession from a new point of view. From the heart.

That's what love has to do with it. In these pages, you'll see what I mean.

CHAPTER 2

The Sacred Trust That Is HR

In the last chapter I talked about the sacred responsibility that goes along with being an HR professional. Now I'm going to take this idea one step further: As an HR leader, you can cultivate a deep trust—a confidence—that sets you apart from everyone else in the company. Maybe even from everyone else in your community. When it comes to the vital importance of keeping your own counsel, there is more at stake in your position than in that of any minister, priest, rabbi, imam, lawyer, or CPA in town. You hold more in your hands than even your CEO. Why? Because the information that you hold in confidence has multidimensional implications for the company, its future prospects, its growth potential, and its position in the marketplace, and, last but certainly not least, for the effect that all this has on the personal life of every one of your employees.

When you go into HR, you must realize that, first and foremost, you are responsible for people's livelihoods. The decisions you make determine people's futures. Every day you make plans that affect individuals on the most intimate levels. Every time you choose between one candidate and another, the decision you make sets off a chain of events that determines the rest of both their lives—even that of the candidates you never see again because they're not a right fit for your company. You decide whether an employee stays or goes. You decide who gets promoted and who doesn't. You decide who gets a raise and who doesn't. By establishing the compensation guidelines or advising management, you influence who gets a generous raise and who doesn't. And you make all these decisions in a larger context of understanding the internal structures and secret plans of the company as a whole.

If you're doing your job well—and if you're running your career well—you are going to know a lot. And you're going to know it before almost everyone else does. You're going to hear what businesses your company might be getting into or out of. You will be one of the first to know when a plant will be opening or when a plant will be closing. Maybe your company is going to stop making a certain product. These are all important things, and you are going to know them before almost everyone else you know—before the people you have lunch with, the people you meet in the hallways, all those people who are making the comfortable assumption that their job is safe. And you have to smile and chat over your sandwich and iced tea, all the while knowing a Big Secret that's going to turn their whole world upside down.

But you're not ready to say anything. You are bound by the SEC to say nothing to anyone until you're ready to say something to everyone. These are the moral and ethical filaments of your calling. The good news is that most days you will not be facing such a crisis. But there may come a day when you're face-to-face with your most closely held principles, and you must also represent the corporate conscience to senior leadership that isn't necessarily in the habit of thinking through the human ramifications of its decisions.

Suppose, for instance, that you know that senior leadership is thinking about abandoning a certain product line. Okay, so far so good. But a year before the company is ready to close the line, the head of that division leaves for a different job and you must fill that spot from the outside. A search is conducted, and you're about to hire a replacement. You're inviting that person to leave a perfectly secure position, uproot his or her family, and require the spouse to change jobs—and to make all of these life-changing moves without knowing about the impending shutdown. What do you do? The line must still run profitably, it needs a leader, but how can you justify the ruination of an otherwise successful career?

Because of your HR perspective, you may be the only one who realizes that personal lives and healthy careers are at stake with this recruitment. So you approach someone in senior leadership who knows as much as you do and shepherd the company through a difficult decision-making process: "Do we really want to do this?" Then you use your position and power to guide the decision-making process in a way that's both smart and right. That is your sacred trust, because only you are in a position to understand and truly know the entire situation and its ripple effects. And by speaking up, you may be the one who is looking out for the company's long-term objectives without compromising a candidate's personal and career interests.

As I write this chapter, the nation is focusing just as much on corporate breaches of trust as it is on dealing with terrorism. Corporate leaders are worrying about it, news anchors are pontificating about it, and shareholders are frantically obsessing about it. And, depending on their relationship with their companies, individual employees are hoping that their trust continues to be well invested. But there's one small change that has resulted from recent SEC rulings that puts these employees at a disadvantage, although they may not be aware of it: Management just can't share its plans with them as freely as it used to. Because many of us worked so hard to cultivate an open-book workplace environment in the 1990s, this is a huge frustration for us. CEOs used to be able to stand up in front of their employees, ballyhoo a fantastic quarter, celebrate everyone's hard work, and predict great expectations for the next quarter. They can't do this anymore. Not unless they have the analysts and the stockholders on the line at the same time.

This makes it very, very hard to establish a relationship of trust with our employees and our communities. Employees don't understand this shift in leadership behavior. Some may regard this sudden lack of information as suspicious, as a disingenuous game of smoke and mirrors with their jobs at stake. How do you reconcile this legal disclosure requirement with your personal HR-from-the-heart philosophy of taking care of both the company's long-term objectives and your employees' personal needs for knowledge, stability, and relative security? Start by making sure that you make no long-term, across-the-board promises that you can't be confident you'll be able to keep. Never promise that your company won't ever have layoffs, for instance. There's just no way you can know that for certain. If you have to have one, you have to have one. But if you're one of the few remaining employers who are promising their workers cradle-to-grave job security, trust will break down in a big hurry when the layoff notices begin.

And, since you have to keep your mouth shut until the company is ready to make a public announcement anyway, make sure you use that extra time wisely. Make sure you've considered all the possible avenues to achieving the company's desired outcomes. As you make your choices and decisions in the predisclosure period, make sure each one can be justified from a fair and rigorous business point of view. Move cautiously, move thoughtfully, and achieve buy-in where you can.

Then, when the time comes to break the bad news companywide and throughout Wall Street, London, and Tokyo, you will know that you will have at least kept the trust.

The Social Side of Secret Keeping

Coworkers talk to each other. Why shouldn't you be among them? If you're in HR, presumably you're a people person, and you will want to have good friends at work. But there are certain boundaries to your relationships with your coworkers that they don't have in their relationships with one another. As the repository of corporate and personal secrets, you must be beyond reproach in terms of the information you hold. You can't afford to be even perceived to be gossiping.

But that doesn't mean your friends will understand this principle. You may be sitting in the cafeteria, enjoying a conversation with your friends. And all of a sudden someone asks you a question that you can't answer: Are we going to have a layoff? How much does so-and-so make? You, of course, say, "That's privileged information and I can't share it with you." But now there's a strain in the friendship, and one or both of you is embarrassed.

This is why I appreciate my friends in HR so much. We know not to ask each other those kinds of questions. And, if we do ask them, it's not because we're angling for gossip. We may be trying to hire the same kind of person and need to compare information for business reasons.

Unfortunately, the flip side of having the inside scoop is that it also sets you apart in some people's eyes as being unapproachable or being somehow above and apart from the rest of your coworkers. I can't tell you how many lunch tables I've approached where people were laughing and telling jokes until the moment I sat down. What? You have no sense of humor just because you're in HR? I've even been with people who use a curse word, look at me, and then say, "Oh! I'm sorry!"

We're not sacred. Our responsibility in HR is. The day that we become holier-than-thou is the day we have to start working very hard to put the human back in our HR work.

CHAPTER 3

Six Essential Ingredients of Every Great HR Career

I was once invited to speak at a *Business 2.0* gathering with a distinguished panel of speakers on the subject "Leading During Turbulent Times." During the question-and-answer session, I was asked the question: "What do people really want from their jobs now that the dot-com bubble has burst?" I answered that I thought that most people just really want to make a difference in their work. They want to add value, but they also want to *feel* valued. The response I got from the audience was both unexpected and dismaying: "It's so refreshing to hear such people-oriented thoughts coming from an HR person!" The meeting moderator herself went on to say that she had always thought of HR people as usually pretty cold, cut-and-dried, and black-and-white. I, of course, thought: "After all these years we're still giving that impression!?"

Many business executives think that the HR person is there to tell them why they can't do the things they want to do. This bad rap is largely created by the fact that management depends on HR to make sure it's in compliance with employment laws and company policies, most of which leave no room for anything but a cut-and-dried, black-and-white approach. So if you're doing your job, it's possible that you're saying no to people on a regular basis. When you're in charge of policies and procedures, it's natural that you get viewed as the enemy of creativity, inspiration, and innovation. If you're saying, "no, no, no" all the time, you are going to be the person your coworkers least like to work with. What a drag!

The good news is this: It doesn't have to be that way. You can stay within employment laws and company policies and procedures and still find creative ways to build a lively, dynamic, exciting, and profitable workplace where people love their work. And as a result, you can cultivate a situation where your department is regarded as the place where great ideas are put into practice.

When people understand that HR is a place where *yes* can happen, it's much easier for them to hold the function in higher esteem. I love what I do every day. That's mainly because I thoroughly understand that no business would exist, no business would be able to make any profits, no business would be able to deliver to its customers, if it didn't have—and keep—precisely the right people in place. People are the drivers of business success. Just one person—the right person—can make a great positive difference in the company's long-term prospects. Conversely, one wrong person can bring the organization down. For better or worse, that person could be anyone on your staff. It could even be you.

Determining whether your relationship with your company is a positive or negative experience begins with the choices you make when you say yes to the employment opportunity. People understandably think that HR professionals are experts in their own careers. But, as you may have already found, when they are faced with the desperate need to find a job, any job, in order to make that mortgage payment and feed their children, many well-intentioned, intelligent people (including seasoned HR professionals) will jump at a job offer, completely ignoring the inner voice that's saying, "Um . . . maybe this company isn't quite right for you."

So what are the essential ingredients of an opportunity that will allow a dedicated, talented HR professional to find happiness and fulfillment?

A Culture Match

As we have already discussed, I have discovered that if you find the right environment, one in which you are appreciated for who you are and for your skills, contentment will follow. It must be a culture you don't have to adapt to. You must be comfortable from the minute you walk in the door. That's the company for you.

At Southwest Airlines, it took me about six months to finally believe, "They want me for who I am." It was a place where I could be myself. Southwest wants people who have a good sense of humor, who can speak out, who can contribute good ideas, and who can deliver results. Those are all things that come naturally to me.

When the time came for me to look for another job (thirteen years later!), I found the same mix at Yahoo! At Yahoo!, you have to hit the ground running. When you get in here, you're expected to speak your mind without waiting for an invitation to do so. Your ideas are valued. Your results are valued. Your ability to work as a team is valued. And everything is done very, very fast.

A Passion Match

Are you actually *interested* in the product or service that your company is providing its customers? If you work for Office Max or Office Depot, does office equipment excite you? Do you relish the thought that all those pens, Post-its, and home fax machines are helping people achieve independence via their own small home-based businesses? If you work for AFLAC or GEICO, do you appreciate the fact that the insurance your company provides to its customers gives them that added measure of security as they deal with the uncertainties of modern life? Are you more fascinated by scientific protocol? Maybe you should be working at a laboratory. Do you love cars? Manufacturers and dealerships need HR. Are you totally turned on by Hollywood? Those big production companies need HR. Find what ignites your passion and connect your HR professionalism to that.

A Values Match

If the company is providing a product or service you don't believe in, if it has a business model you don't believe in, if you can't support what the company stands for, if you don't like the environment, if you're not motivated by the mission, you're always going to feel frustrated there. And perhaps your response to those issues will be to deaden your inner drive to be fabulous. I listen to those sad and shocking news stories about companies that were caught doing irresponsible, even criminal, things. And I want to ask: What was the chief HR person thinking? Yes, it's possible that even the most dynamic, seat-at-the-table HR person may not be privy to all the secret, underhanded schemes of some of the company's senior leadership. But when the activity is fundamentally linked to the way the business makes money, the HR chief must have known *something*. When you know something and it flies in the face of your closely held principles, eventually you're going to have to ask yourself, "Okay, so what do I do about it?" Don't underestimate the importance and long-term impact of your answer to that question.

A People Match

What kinds of people work at your company? Does the company reward high-quality, ethical behavior? Has it established a culture from the very top that attracts passionate, energetic, dedicated, and smart people? Your own dynamic career plan requires you to find companies where people have healthy relationships with one another and their extended communities, where they're all there for the same reason—which is to make the business better. You can have a wildly diverse population of thousands of employees from all different walks of life—in fact, from all over the world. But you can still be unified by one single healthy principle: "We're all here to cooperate with and respect one another and to make this business as great as it can be!"

A Purpose Match

Does your vision of the purpose of HR match that of your CEO? I have heard this from other HR professionals more times than I'd like: "I can't get any support from my CEO," or "My CEO isn't interested in people issues." This is a really interesting problem, because what CEO hasn't said publicly at one time or another, "People are this company's greatest asset"? The CEO will say, "People are irreplaceable"; "Without people we wouldn't have our product"; "Passion makes all the difference." But the CEO's actions say the opposite. You must have a CEO who genuinely values and respects the role that HR and all the people in the company play in pushing the business objectives forward.

Community with Your HR Colleagues

This is one final element of an extraordinary HR career. You can't go it alone. You have to have insight and input from other people who have been in your shoes. Knowing your fellow HR leaders in town and being active in such organizations as the Society for Human Resource Management (SHRM) will give you access to some of the best minds in HR, locally, in the country, and even around the world. I may not be the sharpest knife in the drawer, but thanks to my participation in SHRM and many formal and informal groups over twenty-five years, I *know* some of the sharpest knives in the drawer. Sometimes they can help me when I need help. And sometimes I have just the thing, the idea, the procedure, the approach that they need. Your community may start out as just a local, after-work gang of buddies bending one another's ears. Before you know it, you'll be on a national stage talking to thousands about that solution you've become famous for developing. And it will all have begun with a single phone call to another HR person across town, "Hey, want to get together after work and knock around this problem I've been having? I could use your advice."

CHAPTER 4

Sure It Looks Great, But Does It Fit?

HR may be sacred, but it doesn't have to be serious—at least, not all the time. How much joy you feel free to bring to your job and to the workplace on a daily basis is *the essential question of fit* that almost all of us overlook in our job searches—at least at the beginning of our careers. As recruiters, we know the importance of hiring for fit. But as job seekers ourselves, it's tempting to overlook the issue of whether we personally would fit in a prospective new job. I've discovered over the years that having the ability to laugh out loud and be myself is a cultural nonnegotiable for me. It took me a while to understand that, and even longer to be confident that I could find such a job opportunity. But when the opportunity finally came my way, I was able to look back and wonder how I could ever have settled for less than the perfect fit— the fit where I am able to be my absolutely most joyous, laughing, smiling self and still be respected for the HR professional that I am.

When I finished my MBA program back in the mid-1970s, there was a very popular book out, *Dress for Success*, by John T. Molloy. The first edition was for men. But before too long, the follow-up book *Dress for Success for Women* appeared in the stores. And thus began a period of four or five years in which everyone—men and women—marched into their offices resplendent in brown, gray, blue, or black suits (khaki or seersucker in the summer), complete with white shirt and snappy little silk foulard tie. As white-collar workers, we were all pretty much the same, safe in the knowledge that if we stood out, it wouldn't be because we looked like the proverbial sore thumb. Any standing out we did would, we hoped, be because of our merit, our performance, our excellence.

I'm sure you've heard somewhere in your distant past that your smile is your most important accessory. That's true. But it goes beyond that: Your ability to be yourself in your workplace environment is your most important resource for your personal excellence. And for me, that means feeling free to smile and laugh without worrying that each little grin, each moment of fun and whimsy may be somehow shaving away my credibility. It took a little extra post-MBA education for me to understand that.

When you're out of school for the first time, getting that new job is the most important thing on your mind. Armed with my fresh MBA, I was ready for the search. One of the first companies I interviewed with was a large defense contractor. It was a marathon interview. I was there all day long, meeting with a succession of people well past 4:30. At the end of the process, I was told unceremoniously by the last person to assess my abilities and potential: "I don't think you would fit in here." That floored me. Why wouldn't I fit? I was nice. I was friendly. I get along with just about everyone. I had my foulard tie.

His answer: "You smile too much."

Excuse me? How does someone smile too much? How do you not smile when you're introducing yourself to new people? How do *I* not smile? That's part of who I am. How could I work at a place where people didn't appreciate smiling? Was it possible that all the companies I would be interviewing with would object to me in this fundamental way? What had I gotten myself into?

I was at least able to put my little foulard tie to good use before long. My first big job was with National Sharedata, a high-tech company providing services to twenty-five banking data centers. We were expected to behave and dress the way bankers were expected to behave and dress in the 1970s. Basic culture principles prevailed: Money is serious business. No smiling. No laughing.

I didn't last long. I quickly moved on to my second job. This one was with Mary Kay Cosmetics. I was able to leave my little banker's suit behind me, but I still had to dress like someone I wasn't: like I had just stepped out of *Vogue* magazine. Nails polished, make-up refreshed many times during the day. At National Sharedata, if you wore red shoes, you put your career in serious jeopardy. At Mary Kay, those red shoes were great. But unless your toenails were equally snazzy, you'd better keep those shoes on.

One day (surprise surprise) I was laughing out loud in the hall-way—I mean, really, really loudly. My boss at the time, who was very well intentioned and only wanted the best for me, took me aside and kindly said, "You're so much fun to be around, and I really enjoy working with you. But when you laugh out loud in the hall, people are going to think you're not very professional. You just need to tone it down a little bit."

She thought she was doing the right thing to help me in my career. But the cumulative effect of these experiences was to teach me to suppress the laughter, humor, and joyousness that feed my soul and fuel my love for HR. Basic culture principles prevailed: Red shoes good. Manicures expected. Raucous laughter bad.

I learned many wonderful things at Mary Kay, but eventually it was time to move on. My next job was at Recognition Equipment, Inc. (which became Recognition International), a high-tech sales, service, and electronics manufacturing company whose major products included document imaging and scanning, high-speed data transport, and data entry equipment. The old banker's uniform from National Sharedata worked well in this setting. The only problem was that *dressing* the part was easier than *behaving* the part. One day I was having a staff meeting in my office with the door closed, and something had struck us as funny. So we were laughing our heads off (are you picking up a pattern here?). My boss opened the door, leaned in, and said, "I guess if you're having this much fun in here, you're not doing very much work." And then he closed the door. That just sucked all the life right out of the room; all that fun we were having dissipated like a broken spell.

Over the early years of my career, I had learned to be a chameleon, and I could change with every environment as necessary. What I really needed to know was how to find an environment that didn't expect me to change at all.

So, to put it mildly, it was quite a culture shock when I found my way into Southwest, where the boss, Herb Kelleher, was featured in a major business magazine dressed like Elvis. Herb laughs even louder than I do! I spent so much time worrying, "What do they expect of me? what do they expect of me?" that it took me some time to realize—and then believe—that what Southwest really wanted was for me to be happy and be myself! But one day I was standing in yet another hallway laughing out loud with two other women. And instead of subtle digs and kind corrections, this is what we heard from a coworker: "I'm going to have a party and invite all three of you. You're all known for your big bursts of laughter. And it's so endearing!"

What a revelation! I was valued at Southwest just for being myself. And the thirteen years that followed flew by in a blink.

When you find the things you really like to do in an environment where you're really comfortable, your career loses the work aspect and becomes a natural part of your life. We spend so much time focusing on building our marketable skills and making ourselves irresistible to companies we think we want to work for that we leave an essential part of ourselves behind—our passion and our heart. It's terribly sad that so many people decide on a career that they expect will be "hot" throughout their working lives or try to change themselves to fit into the wrong environment because they think a particular company is an important "ticket to punch," and never find their passion or find a workplace environment in which they can really blossom.

If we, as HR professionals, can't link career and passion for ourselves, how can we expect to be able to do it for the employees of our organizations? One of the parts of HR that I get the most joy out of is helping people find the absolutely right environment in which to do the things they enjoy doing. When they find that, they're going to be successful, and they're going to make enough money no matter what.

Fortunately, we in HR are lucky. Every company in every industry needs the HR function. So when it comes to seeking out an environment we can invest our passion in, the world is wide open to us. Do you like retail? Seek out retail. Do you like nonprofit organizations? Go there. Do you like project work and the ability to develop creative solutions to specific situations? Consider consulting. Would you rather wear sandals to work than oxfords? Maybe a relaxed resort environment is more your speed.

Cause, culture, coworker relationships, contributions to the world . . . all those elements make up your career path in a profound way. So don't just look at the job description. Factor all those details into your decision to accept a job offer, even if the details seem as trivial to your inner adult as expected behaviors or dress codes.

Emerson wrote: "Mistrust all enterprises that require new clothes." He wasn't worrying so much about helping you save money. He was thinking about saving you time—the time of your life. Every second you spend trying to be something—or someone—you're not already is a second you'll never have back again.

CHAPTER 5

Not Everyone Will Be
President of Your Fan Club

People who choose HR as a career are usually attracted by the first word in HR: human. "Aha!" we think. "Here is our chance to take what we know and care about (namely, people and helping them) and do it in a business setting." The stronger you feel that human connection between the HR function and business life, the more *called* you may say you are to your profession.

The more *called* you may feel, the less you're going to like this news: You will make enemies. At the very least, some people won't like you. There will be some people who will resent you. And some of them may never forget "what you did to them." In fact, some of those people may not hold anything against you personally. They'll just despise you generally. They might have had a run-in with HR fifteen years ago—long before you ever came on the scene—and now you're guilty by association.

Unfortunately, some areas in HR are more prone to grudges and grudge bearers than others. No matter what you do within the HR profession, you are the caretaker of people's dreams and ambitions. But if you are in certain functions, it may be part of your job description to say *no* more often than *yes*. If you're in compensation and benefits, for instance, you may have to say no to a supervisor who is fighting to keep a valued employee who has just been offered a huge salary increase by a competing company. If you're in employment, for every person you hire and make the happiest person in the world, you are making many, many more people very unhappy by telling them they didn't get the job. If you have a fully developed internal promotion process, all those people who didn't get the new opportunity may be thinking to themselves, "I didn't get the job because this HR person doesn't like me."

Or you may have a supervisor who is absolutely committed to terminating an employee, but who, according to your progressive discipline procedures, hasn't given the employee sufficient notice to enable him to correct the problem performance. So you have to disappoint the supervisor. The employee may never know that you saved his career at the last minute. But the supervisor may long remember how you threw a monkey wrench into her plans to get rid of an undesirable worker.

Or you may be in a key HR position at your town's most important employer. As far as the local community is concerned, you are at least as powerful in many ways as your CEO. You have more power, even, than the local guy who just won a multimillion-dollar lottery. Instead of sitting on a big bag of cash, you're sitting on a big bag of secrets: job opportunities, growth or downsizing plans, and a number of other details that directly influence people's peace of mind and their mortgage payments. That great job opening that you don't tell your best friend about, or that massive layoff plan that you don't tell the business page of your local newspaper about, can make you very unpopular among your friends and neighbors.

All these scenarios are common in any HR career. But I think the HR professionals who are most at risk for making enemies are not the ones who displease and disappoint. The ones who make enemies are the ones who underestimate the extent of their own influence and power. But there are ways in which you can get your job done, contribute to the healthy growth of your company and community, and maintain relationships that are built on trust and respect.

■ *Underpromise and overdeliver.* Don't set up false expectations. When you say yes to everyone indiscriminately, you're eventually going to get the reputation of being incompetent and unreliable, and—even worse—you'll lose your credibility. Deliver more than you promise to deliver, and you'll build respect for the overall HR department and market your own trustworthiness throughout the company.

■ *Go for the win/win solution.* Avoid saying a flat no whenever you can. If you can't grant the request as it was presented to you, try to identify the real need behind the expressed request and fill the need instead. Go for the win/win. Perhaps a supervisor comes to you with a request that you significantly increase her secretary's salary. But that increase is absolutely beyond the compensation and benefits plan for support staff grades. Don't just say a flat no. Find an alternative, creative solution. Can you transfer the secretary to a professional track, so that she will be able to qualify for a higher salary range or a more rapid rate of increase? Can you assign the secretary to a development program that promises long-term growth and potential, as opposed to the immediate reward of a salary increase? Can you move this person to a supervisory or training position where he can guide and direct other employees?

■ *Don't get personal.* When you discover that suddenly you're someone's enemy, look back at the series of events that led up to this strain in your relationship. You'll probably discover that somewhere along the way, you dropped your professional role and got personal. When you deal with people's livelihoods, it gets very personal for them. You are the only professional who is experienced at keeping HR issues businesslike. Non-HR people are amateurs at separating business issues from their personal paycheck issues. Give them the benefit of your experience and professionalism. Ultimately it will be your cool head that serves both their interests and the company's.

■ *Don't take it personally.* One of my colleagues at Southwest taught me this one. I was sharing an experience that I considered to be a personal assault. She said that even though it felt personal, it wasn't. It was business. I sometimes have to remind myself of that fact. During the hiring boom of the late 1990s, we had to work harder and harder to find employees who met our high standards and were willing to work at relatively low hourly rates. No matter how much we cranked up our efforts, the recruiting staff was producing less-than-desirable results. Our senior team decided to be "helpful" by calling for a complete review of our hiring processes to see if an outsider could help us see what we were missing. You'd have to be superhuman not to take this personally—and the last time I checked, there were no superhumans on my team. We were just doing a superhuman job. So we were really offended by this implication from above that somehow we weren't doing everything we could do. But, as my colleague reminded us, it was just business.

■ *Don't take sides and don't seek vengeance.* We're all human, and there may be people inside your company who bring out your worst impulses. Just as it's important that you do not show favoritism, it's also important that you do not give in to a natural impulse to retaliate against someone who has hurt you on the job. I've seen HR people go after people with the attitude, "I'm going to get that person!" Believe me, it never works out. Even if you win and that person quits (or is terminated), word spreads, and you'll never be totally trusted again. When that happens, you might as well leave, too.

■ *Take a stand and do the right thing.* Actually, this approach to your work may make you enemies. If you're taking a stand in favor of a value or principle, some people are bound to take it very personally, to believe that you're taking a stand *against* them. That can't be helped. If you stand up for your values, if you stand up against truly toxic and cruel managers, you will continue to be able to take the most important stand of all—the stand that you take in front of the mirror. True, you work with others. But you have to live with yourself.

■ *Be your own best example.* Model forgiveness and, to a reasonable extent, forgetfulness. Build a workplace environment in which people are expected to make mistakes, in which it's safe to be human, and in which most errors are treated philosophically as learning experiences that everyone will benefit from. Cut others slack, and they'll return the favor when you slip up. Which you will do.

Stay true to your values and use your profession to help grow a company in which all the employees can thrive. You'll still make enemies now and then. But you can control who they are and how many they are.

CHAPTER 6

Great Relationships Are More About What You Give Than What You Get

Here it is in a nutshell: Find out what the people in your life want and give it to them—the way they want it.

This may seem like such a basic piece of advice, and you may be asking yourself, "Why is she taking the time, ink, and paper to deliver such a kindergarten-level rule for getting along with people?" It seems strange, I know, to go into this basic principle in a book for adults, but I've seen too many careers crash and burn because people didn't mindfully build relationships (with people above them, below them, and all around them) that worked. When people fail in a job, it's usually not because they don't know something or because they don't do their job well. It's because they fail to build good relationships. And this failure knows no maturity, experience, or success level. CEOs fail for this reason, and new graduates fail for this reason. But what's saddest for me is seeing HR people who don't get it themselves. They should know better and should be coaching others in this strength.

You can go to all the leadership and motivation courses in the world, but if you don't stop to find out what's in the hearts of the people you're dealing with, you might as well ask for your tuition money back. No other trick, no other technique, no other sure-fire method of getting along with others will work until you have integrated that one fundamental principle into every encounter and relationship that you have.

What All Bosses Will Want From You, No Matter Who They Are

The biggest mistake many people make is assuming that the way to get along with their boss is to do a good job. Yes, of course, you're expected to do a good job—well, a *great* job. But just as important, if not more important, bosses want you to serve their agenda and the agenda of the enterprise. And where you are concerned, item number one on that agenda is to have a cooperative staffer who isn't an opinionated pain in the derriere, even if the boss is wrong. That's where I ran into trouble early in my career.

Fresh out of grad school (and after plenty of leadership courses), I entered the work world fully expecting bosses to be perfect—above all possible human flaws and infinitely wise. My first boss quickly demonstrated how wrong I was, and I wasn't shy about using every instance of disagreement to try to convince him how wrong *he* was. Looking back, I realize now that I learned a lot from him in our short (and I mean *short*) relationship. He knew a lot about HR, and he gave me the opportunity to learn as much as I could, or would, from him. But our relationship was predictably brief, and I set out again on my search for the perfect boss.

After several disappointments in a variety of companies, I found the perfect boss at Southwest. But within my first year there, she left the company. And she was replaced by a (gasp!) imperfect boss. Ann Rhoades came in and immediately wanted to do things that I thought were just plain wrong-headed for the company. And, of course, I thought my opinions were infallible. In my mission to do "a good job," I told her my opinions. Her ideas either weren't right for the company culture, or the company had already considered and dismissed them in the past. Within her first two days at the company, we had three really big arguments. I put my head down on my desk and sighed in despair, "I can't believe this is happening again!"

And then I realized, "I can manage my relationship with my boss." Okay, I thought, if she comes in tomorrow and says, "The grass is pink," I'm going to agree with her. Of course, it never quite came to that extreme, but I was prepared to go there if I had to. So I built a new habit: Instead of saying no to her ideas right away, I would make a serious effort to consider her suggestions and to prepare to put her ideas into practice. And then I would return to her with some other suggestions and say, "I tried your suggestion, but it didn't play out as well as we hoped. Here are some other approaches. Which one do you think would work best for the company?"

She would choose one of the suggestions. It was what I would have chosen anyway, but *she* made the choice. And she knew that she had a supportive staffer whose mission was to be a team contributor, not to win an argument. After I did this several times, she learned to trust me and to realize that I could make good decisions as well. So she quit arguing with me and started asking me for my input. The early days of our relationship were tense, and I can only imagine how it seemed to her to have a new direct report challenge everything she suggested. But eventually she learned that I could be trusted to serve her agenda and do the right thing for the company. And so she gave me more latitude, we became friends, and we could then look back on our doubtful beginnings and laugh about it.

Find out what your boss's agenda is. Trust that he or she was selected for that role because of talent that was obvious to the leaders of the company. And if it's not illegal or immoral or the wrong thing to do in other ways, go along with that agenda. Your personal agenda is not more important than your boss's (no matter how chowder-headed you think your boss is). Develop a great relationship, even a friendship, with your boss, and you'll be creating new opportunities for yourself to grow and lead in the near future.

What All Coworkers Want, No Matter Who They Are

Coworkers want you to respect and understand the fact that they may not be motivated by the same things that you are. Everyone has a unique set of drives, ambitions, values, fears, and motivations. True, your coworkers may want to do a great job, but the fuel that fires their engines may very well be different from what fires yours. In fact, they may not be as motivated as you are at any given point of their careers or lives. But that doesn't mean that they're bad employees or that you need to turn up the heat. To get what you want from your coworkers, you must understand what they want. And if it's not within your power or part of your role to provide it to them, at the very least you can respect their differences.

I ran into trouble early in my career in this area as well. I expected all my coworkers to want the same things I did. I assumed that they would be as passionate about what they did as I was. I thought that they wanted to work hard, deliver results, get ahead, climb the ladder, and achieve career success. And mostly it was true.

But there was one coworker who simply didn't like me. How could that be? I was nice to her. I tried to share everything I had learned on the job with her. (I even gave her tips on how to get along with the boss!) I tried to save her from a few embarrassing moments. I thought, "She should love me, right?" As I began to realize that she wasn't my biggest fan, I tried harder to win her over. This only made things worse.

I finally gave up and asked my boss if he had any idea what was wrong. He told me that I came on too strong, that I was coming off as a "know it all" and had intimidated her. The very fact that I was so good at my job, he said, made it difficult for her to work with me, and therefore I shouldn't let her know how competent I was. *I* was the one who needed to change, he said, and I should back off.

My mistake was an innocent one: I assumed that she had the same goals, the same standards, and the same work ethic that I did. In fact, I assumed that she had the same work *style* that I did, and I assumed that anything different was somehow a mistake. It didn't cross my mind that she had an entirely different set of perspectives, values, habits, and approaches to work—and that they were just as legitimate as mine. The good news is that once I did back off, as my boss had requested, I relaxed, and she relaxed, and our working relationship improved significantly.

Not everyone has the same goals, hopes, dreams, work styles, and objectives that you do. Some are working hard because they have to, not because they're especially passionate about their work. Some won't work as hard as you do. Some won't *look* as if they're working as hard as you do. We're all different, but that difference can get lost in the uniform culture of a workplace environment with shared goals, objectives, mission, values, and deliverables. The best coworkers are those who have skills that are different from ours. We must learn to appreciate opposite personalities. If you're a big-picture-oriented extrovert, it's vital that you see the important contributions of the introvert with a deeply analytical mind and perhaps plodding methods. The critical personality with a negative streak might be the first to discover that multimillion-dollar flaw in the otherwise promising business plan. The creative genius might take forever turning in the budget, but once those funds are allocated, the innovations she creates with the money may carry the company forward into a new era. A team with diverse talents is a strong team, and a team of clones is weak.

It's nice to have bosses and coworkers who like you and think you're a terrific person. But it's essential to have bosses and coworkers who *trust* you with their most cherished values and motivations. When they know that their dreams and fears are safe with you (as yours are with them), the work will take care of itself.

CHAPTER 7

Pull Up a Chair . . .
(How to Know You're Really Ready for a Seat at the Table)

These days it's all the rage in HR to talk about finally achieving that "seat at the table." I haven't been to an HR conference or read a book on the future of the profession in the past decade that didn't include a reference to the idea that a true HR leader must actively seek out a more strategic role. It's commonly accepted wisdom that if HR is present at *the table*, then HR has truly arrived in the power circles of a company. Or, more important, it means that an enlightened organization has realized that the success of the business is dependent not only on financial or operational performance, but also on the human element of the business.

While we're all so fluent in talking about that seat at the table, most of us really don't have a solid idea of what the table is or what to do once we get there. I know I didn't. And without the benefit of a little additional understanding, I stubbed my toe, got my feelings hurt, and had to invest some extra time and energy in achieving the respect and stature that I thought automatically came with the territory.

When I first campaigned for and eventually was granted that seat at the table, I thought I was "in." I was surprised to find that the group wasn't at all accepting of me at first. Just because I was there didn't mean that I had earned the seat.

I blew it at the very first meeting. As painful as the memory still is, I would like to share my story, hoping that it may keep others from stepping into the same trap. Before the first meeting of the year—my first meeting—our chairman sent us a memo outlining our agenda. We were going to spend the day brainstorming strategic issues. How should we grow? Should we acquire? Should we consider new markets? Should we change our niche? Were different strategies needed? What factors would impede our growth? What were our customer service issues? Could we attract the talent we needed in order to grow? Where would we find the leaders we needed? What might the government do that would jeopardize our business in the future? What other external factors might come up?

Wow . . . I had hit the big time! I had gotten where I was because I was a person who could bring about change, who had an opinion, who wasn't afraid to take risks, who challenged traditional thinking, who had innovative ideas, who could anticipate the future. I falsely assumed that this was why I was invited to the table. Yet, in fact, I felt unprepared to answer many of the questions the chairman posed. I hadn't researched new market possibilities. I didn't know whether a change in strategy or operational procedures or new equipment made financial sense. But I *did* feel that I could make an impact on the talent and leadership issues. And so, I reasoned, that was where I would contribute real substance, real value. So in the few days I had before the meeting, I read books and articles about future trends in my industry and HR. I made a list of provocative ideas that I could interject into the discussion. I was determined not to sit there with my mouth shut. I was going to make an impact at my first meeting. I had to add something that wouldn't be there if HR weren't at the table.

I arrived, ready to be a *player*. My first mistake was that I sat in the wrong chair. I didn't know that the CFO always sat at the left hand of the CEO. I thought the CEO would sit at the head of the table, not the middle. I got the evil eye from several teammates before the meeting even started. Every other meeting I had had with these folks, my friends, had been lighthearted and fun; joking was allowed. But with this same group in this different setting, the rules were different. I cracked a joke, and no one laughed. Uh-oh. This meeting was serious. As the discussion began, I looked for my opportunity. Where could I make a pertinent point? Finally, I found a chance to jump in. I don't remember what I said, but I do remember the utter silence, the stares, the icy cold feeling. *No talking allowed from the new kid!* That's what it felt like. It was the longest day of my life. I knew I had blown it, but I didn't know why.

After the meeting, I met with several people who had been at the meeting and asked what the rules were. I was utterly mystified. I had been at this company for eleven years. I knew these people. How could I have gotten it so badly wrong so soon? This was the same room, the same table, the same group who had welcomed me as a guest presenter for years. But, ironically, now that I was one of them, I was *less* one of them than I had been before. Finally, I came to understand what my presence meant to them.

First of all, HR had never been at that level before, so my whole function was on a sort of probation, not just me. Second, I wrongly assumed that since I had been invited to be a member of this elite strategic committee, I was also invited to participate immediately at an equal level with those who had been there for ten years. I thought that I had to make my mark right away, at the first meeting. I thought I must speak, contribute, advise, and even drive the discussion whenever I thought it was appropriate—even when the discussion had nothing to do with HR. I assumed that everyone thought I belonged at the table. But in fact, several folks didn't feel that HR had a place on the executive committee at all. I wasn't welcome, and I felt it.

To make matters worse, at the second meeting, I was slated to discuss an issue that I considered to be very important—the issue of domestic partner benefits. Now this is a topic that many people have difficulty discussing in their living rooms, let alone when it is thrown in their faces in an exclusive meeting by the most junior person in the boardroom. And, while I could definitely see the ways in which such a program would add value to the business, those who didn't want to discuss it at all were the last to be open to hearing about how domestic partner benefits would advance overall corporate objectives. I was shot down unceremoniously on my first attempt (but months later succeeded in implementing a very successful program).

That was the very unpromising beginning to my career at the long-coveted table. I should have waited long enough to learn the conventions of this group and to be accepted before digging in on such a controversial issue. And I asked myself many times afterward whether I would have been better off just coming to the table now and then as an invited guest. At least in those circumstances, I had known that I was officially on the program, and that they truly wanted to know what I had to say.

In their book *What Every Successful Woman Knows,* authors Janice Reals Ellig and William J. Morin point out that every company is a composite of different cultures at different levels of the organization. By the time you make it to the proverbial table, there is only one culture—the one defined by the chairman of the board. When you get to this level, everything you do is visible, and the acceptance of behavior that is different from the established norms is virtually nonexistent. Newcomers to boards often fail to adapt to the senior management culture. They get to the table by exhibiting skills as change agents and by standing out. But in this new group, they must first fit in and gain personal credibility, and then maybe they will have a chance of driving the agenda of the enterprise.

Do You Really Want the Headache?

Over the years, I've heard many HR people say that they will take a new HR job only if there is a place for HR on the executive committee or if they report directly to the chairman or CEO. But I never hear people say what they're going to do once they achieve that prominence. It's like all those young women who focus so much on the wedding that they don't have a clue to what marriage is all about. And as with marriage, there are good aspects to the relationship, and there are bad aspects.

Let's start with the good aspects.

- You're there when all the important business and strategic decisions are made, and even some that aren't so strategic. Witnessing the discussion and the thought process that goes into each decision gives you a greater understanding of the company's values and what is important to each leader. You know what the HR issues will be as a result of strategic decisions. That experience is often more valuable than just knowing the end result: the decision itself.

- You will have the chance to address the HR and people ramifications of a decision *before* the decision is solidified. You can create a better, custom HR agenda that will support not only the decision but also the underlying business and financial priorities of the executive team.

- Likewise, you can protect the spirit of your company's HR philosophy if the business decision somehow conflicts with it.

- You can demonstrate the true value of HR to the corporation. You have the chance to develop wonderful working relationships with powerful corporate leaders, find out what their HR issues are, and then create excellent strategies to help them deal with those issues.

- You can help create the company's future by influencing its development decisions early.

- You will have the opportunity to learn the entire business. A seat at the table is like an MBA practicum. You're there when *all* the major issues from *all* the departments are discussed.

These are the negatives:

- You'll be frustrated at a much higher level than you ever were before. The stakes are higher, and people who may be your antagonists will be more deeply invested in their points of view.

- You will be spending more time on work matters. In general, work at this level is far more time-consuming, and there will be more committee assignments that go with this appointment.

- Your personal career and job security will be more exposed. You will be bringing up issues that no one wants to talk about. You will disturb the equilibrium now and then. And you may wear out your welcome.

- Your own mistakes will be much more visible. You'll be exposed to criticism.

- The stakes will be high for you as well. You will be forced to take a stand now and then. You may end up disagreeing with a given course of action. Right or wrong, you must be ready to take the heat—and a hit—now and then.

So how do you know whether you're ready for this exposure and responsibility? If you can answer yes to these questions, you are ready to give it a try:

- Can I hide my hurt feelings? (Other advice books may tell you you're ready when your feelings no longer get hurt. Who are they kidding?)

- Can I deal with conflict?

- Can I take on tough issues bravely without backing down?

- Am I able to make good business arguments in favor of or against certain proposed actions?

- Can I find good, diplomatic solutions to conflicts? Am I creative in finding ways in which more people can get what they want?

- Have I stopped looking up to my executive team? Do I believe that I have the right to be there without feeling that I'm an impostor on borrowed time? Am I ready to adapt my style to the culture of the new group? Am I patient enough to make the effort to fit into the group and gain credibility?

If you have answered no to some of those questions, don't feel bad. This doesn't mean that you've failed or that you've fallen short of some ideal measure. The important thing is to be where you can best deliver to your customer. And very often you may have an advantage if you make focused presentations to the executive team several times a year as a specifically invited expert. Quit worrying about whether you're there every time, or whether you report to the most powerful person. Set your sights on getting invited frequently and on being heard. That's where your power will lie.

CHAPTER 8

. . . And Have a Seat
(What to Do Once You Finally Get There!)

So you've finally been invited to join the executive committee! And
you're ready for the challenge! Congratulations! So now what do you
do? As we saw in the last chapter, the last thing you want to do is to
start flapping your yap and alienating your new teammates with ill-
advised comments and suggestions. Please, oh please, don't bring the
language of HR to the table. You need to adapt, earn trust, gain credibility, and make a real difference for the business. Unless you have the
great good luck of joining a newly formed executive team as one of
the original members, you will be entering an already established
group—a group that has its own shared memories, routines, patterns,
and even an unwritten pecking order. It is very much like a newly
adopted child entering an already established family. And, as with an
already established family, there may be a few members who aren't all
that wild about your presence there. There are so many subterranean
dynamics that go on in any group—let alone in a group of powerful,
ambitious superachievers, like an executive committee. It's easy to

take the wrong steps if you take on too much too quickly. The smart new arrival knows to hang back just a little, watch the dynamics, and start recruiting allies one by one behind the scenes.

Find a trusted confidante, a mentor who knows the ropes and is supportive and positive so that you have someone to run things by before taking them to the table. Ask that person the important questions that will most likely support your successful acceptance into the team: What are the most pressing issues that the team is dealing with right now? How does the team expect me to contribute? What should be my immediate agenda? Who is making an impact? Who seems to engender the confidence and respect of the group? Learn from those leaders.

Look for something that you can safely achieve right away. Try to accomplish a couple of quick wins as soon as possible—wins that benefit everyone, where no one is the loser. Find a process that you can fix, and then fix it. Take on a small assignment or task, and bring it to closure successfully. That halo effect will buy you a little extra time at the beginning, so that you can then sit back and take the time to learn the things you need to know and to establish deeper relationships in order to further your longer-term goal of being accepted and trusted as an effective, respected business partner at the table.

Know your place. Understand what you should talk about. Understand when to keep quiet. Focus on business objectives rather than HR programming. Create your own agenda of HR issues that are related to important business trends and report on them regularly. If you can address issues related to the talent that will be needed if the organization is to gain a sustainable competitive advantage, and show the results, you will get your share of the discussion and add value: attraction and retention of high performers, filling hard-to-hire jobs, the efficacy of your compensation program, building leadership bench strength, and creating a workplace that energizes and retains the best talent. But don't interfere with topics that don't affect—or are not affected by—human resources. This is your time to sit and learn.

Learn how to best communicate to the group. You will quickly see what method works best—a PowerPoint presentation, being able to illustrate a concept on the white board, or telling a good story to illustrate your point. I have seen many people blow it by providing too much information. And some by not providing enough.

Develop and enjoy your internal role in the group. No matter what your level in the company is, to the executive team you are always the HR generalist. Even though you may have devoted your entire career to getting out of the generalist role, this is an opportunity to relish. You'll be the most senior HR strategic partner for this group. Work one-on-one with each member to help develop the leadership teams, address people issues, and drive the agenda. This will foster the team's understanding of both the basics and the more advanced concepts of HR as they pertain to the company and its future. This is a great opportunity for you to keep honing your own HR expertise and to set the example for your team members.

Likewise, as you get more comfortable in the group, it will be your responsibility to make sure that the team is a high-performing one.

Take the lead in creating team development and conflict resolution opportunities for this group. Help to establish the rules of engagement. Just as the company as a whole is looking to HR to make sure its employees are equipped to meet their objectives on the job, it is your job as the team HR leader to make sure that the other team members have what they need in order to achieve their objectives.

What we do with our position at the table, when we have the chance, can make a real difference in the success of our organization and the lives of our people. That's what really matters. You can be a source of energy and help the top team achieve higher levels than would otherwise have been possible. You can help the top team abandon old styles of thinking and break through to new levels of performance and understanding. Being part of a high-performance team is truly one of the most rewarding experiences any business or HR leader can have. This kind of team can engage the workforce so that it focuses on clear strategies and delivers results. And this kind of team can create and drive a culture in which people bring their passion and their best talents to work. It can achieve extraordinary performance and growth. It can create a one-of-a-kind sustainable competitive advantage that no one can duplicate. It can create stellar financial performance. It can create business legend.

CHAPTER 9

From the Heart Doesn't Mean from the *Bleeding* Heart

When most people meet me, they very quickly assume they have my number. And for the most part they're right. I've never been one of those inscrutable, dominating executives who win through intimidation and through keeping information to myself. I'm pretty much out there. There is usually a smile on my face. (Why not? I love my work.) I'm genuinely glad to see most people I know through work, and I thrive in environments in which I can greet people with a hug rather than a handshake. I crave the human connection of business, and HR has given me a great platform from which I can help people build their lives while they build the company. In my experience, there's a lot of "feel good" potential about this calling of HR.

But people who think they've sized me up as a pushover or think that I don't understand the hard realities of business are in for a big surprise. And probably not a very pleasant one, either, if those people are on the losing end of going *mano a mano* with me in a business-related face-off. Being a from-the-heart HR professional doesn't mean being a doormat HR professional. You're not doing anyone a favor by giving in, compromising your principles, or compromising your company's potential in the name of protecting feelings or enabling people to stay in jobs that are clearly a poor fit for them.

The right thing to do isn't always the nice thing to do. To be successful in any area of business, and especially in HR, you have to make a lot of tough decisions. We make choices every day that affect people's livelihoods and the well-being of their families. We never *want* to fire people. We never *want* to close down entire plants or operating divisions. But we partner with management in these efforts and often implement these decisions. We want to promote people. We certainly want to be good HR citizens in our communities. If we could somehow manufacture or clone new talent instead of stealing it from our colleagues in the company down the block, we would. To many gifted, heart-felt HR professionals who clearly see the human aspect of the business story, corporate competition—especially when we win at someone else's expense—feels so . . . well, so *dog-eat-dog*.

Here's another way to look at it. Corporate competition is a sport of volunteers, not a trap for victims. Yes, there are rules to this sport. And, yes, your objective is to win, but not at the expense of your self-respect and personal code of morals and ethics. And, yes, every now and then you'll encounter cheaters: players who have their own ideas of what the rules are; people who grab the trophy away from the rightful winners. But what sport doesn't have those? As the HR leader, you are absolutely mandated to be as aggressive a competitor as any other player on the team. But you are also the coach: You're responsible for the training and development of the entire team, and for cultivating a winning spirit. Everyone is prohibited from violating the rules of the competition—the coach even more so.

Even in this era, where it's an exciting and creative challenge to try to arrive at win/win scenarios, in a truly competitive environment there are many losers when someone wins. Of the thousands of people who apply for a job (or of the many who competed with you for your job, for that matter), only one person can actually get the job. What about everyone else? They lost. When you're trying to recruit a true star in your field, you're competing with other employers for that great talent. If you're able to create a compelling package that prevails, great. You win. If you can't, sorry, you lose.

We live and work in a competitive environment every day. And in most everyday situations (especially the ones in which we don't actually know our competitors personally), we can live with the game. It gets really hard, though, when there's a personal element thrown in. Or when you just can't reconcile yourself to the competitive realities of the free-enterprise system.

Yes, it is about winning. But it's not about winning at all costs. Over the years I've met more than a few HR leaders who were originally attracted to the field because they really cared about people, but then had to figure out how to cultivate enough clout and competitiveness to gain the power they thought they needed in order to be effective—and to be respected by the senior team. Suddenly they felt they were at choice points, where they had to choose between what was right and what was strategically expedient. For a variety of reasons—ambition, laziness, or a misguided impression that in order to be successful in the corporate setting, they had to behave like reptiles—they began choosing the strategically expedient. And, as with many other slippery slides of life, once you make that first expedient choice, it gets easier and easier to make the next ones. The harder it is for you to recognize that being a compassionate, humanistic HR leader *is* good competition, the more at risk you are of choosing one extreme over the other. And neither extreme serves either your career or your company well.

If this is a problem for you, you're not alone. It's one of the main reasons why HR isn't given the respect it deserves throughout the corporate world. Here are some basic principles to think about as you consider your own capacity for playing to win.

■ *Competition is a good thing.* It promotes improvement and development of your industry's products and services. It sharpens skills and improves processes. It motivates. It's the breeding ground for change and progress.

■ *There's room for only one Number One.* Except for the Avis rental car company ("We try harder"), I can't think of any competitor that has gotten any mileage out of coming in second. In order to grab that Number One spot, you're going to have to knock whoever already has that spot off the perch.

■ *Competition isn't about hurting anyone, it's about capitalizing on your differentiation.* Few people, unless they're sadistic, relish causing pain. So if you think of the end result of competitiveness as a painful thing, no wonder you aren't motivated to play the game. Capture the loyalty of your customers (both external and internal) through differentiation: What do you offer? How is it different from and/or better than the other choices in the marketplace? How are your customers going to connect emotionally with what your company stands for, as opposed to their other choices?

■ *To be the true winner, you can't play just for the sake of winning.* If you play to win at all costs, your organization will lose that feeling of heart and soul and passion. Even in sports, the teams that win the most know that winning requires more than speed, power, and accuracy. In pregame pep talks, you don't hear coaches rave on about the number of pounds the players can lift. They celebrate the team's vision and mission, and the legacy that the team is about to express and create. From-the-heart HR must create a from-the-heart passion to win.

It's Okay to Steal. And It's Mandatory to Share

One challenge connected with being in HR is the fact that you know your competitors personally. You encounter them at SHRM chapter meetings. You serve on committees with them. You give one another career advice. You catch one another's eye across big circular tables and gesture for the cream pitcher during an interminable lecture on god-knows-what-all. How can you snatch their best talent right out from under them and be able to sleep at night? You can because you must. And you might as well, because they're doing the same thing to you.

While I certainly wouldn't conduct an all-out raid on an organization, I have no problem asking new hires and other employees who else they know who matches my recruiting needs at the moment. That means that as new hires give their two weeks' notice at their current employer, the word is getting around that there may be more opportunities at my company to apply for. So after one new hire, a couple of others from the same company (maybe even the same department) might follow quickly. Do I sleep well at night? You betcha!

Do I like it when other companies do the same to me? Hell, no! But, free enterprise is free enterprise. Only once did I really take offense when this tactic was used against my organization. One of my HR counterparts in another company routinely targeted and siphoned off my best talent. It began to get seriously annoying. So I wrote her a letter asking her to knock it off. She didn't.

She also had a to-the-death philosophy about competition. A few years later, her company was folding. A lot of great talent was going to be hitting the bricks, looking for new work. I contacted her again and offered to hold a special job fair for her employees. Of course, I had a lot to gain from the offer: I could cherry-pick the best of the best (I knew better than anyone else, obviously, what kind of talent was going to be available very soon). So her employees (and by extension, one would think, she herself) would have gained from the opportunities my company would be able to offer them. She turned me down. She was too competitive to give up the fight, even though the fight was over.

Every company in the world is a study in effective competitiveness. Either it's the leader or it's figuring out ways to hone its practices, products, and processes in order to gain market position. In the HR function, perhaps your most valuable competitive edge is that you're the only HR player who truly embraces the great game of competitiveness. When you do that, you're contributing profound value to the company. By helping to improve your company's standing, you're creating opportunities, openings, and stability in your community and industry. Think of all the ways in which that personally benefits the people who are connected with you.

That's about as compassionate as you can get.

CHAPTER 10

Know Your Stuff and Know That You Know Your Stuff
(And Don't Let Anyone Tell You Otherwise)

By the time I finally entered my professional career years, I was unusually well educated for the HR field and for a young woman in the mid-1970s. And I knew it. I knew going in that the more education I had, the lower my barriers to entry would be in a world that was still uneasy about having women in business. So instead of jumping into my working life right after my undergraduate years, I invested more time to get an MBA from the University of North Texas, with a special emphasis on HR (called personnel administration at the time) and industrial relations. That MBA, I knew, would give me a competitive edge against all the nameless, faceless applicants I would be competing with for jobs—at least in my early years—and I would avoid the dreaded question that plagued most women trying to break into the job market in those days, "How fast can you type?"

So it was relatively quick and easy for me to land a position as a personnel administrator at National Sharedata. But the true value of my "book learnin'" became very clear to me on my first day. I didn't know how to use the photocopier.

So I did what anyone would do: I found the first friendly (and female) face and asked her to show me how to use it. And she did, but not without making a disparaging—but to the point—observation about my fancy education. I found out not too much later that she had been one of my nameless and faceless competitors for this job. Despite her inside track and real-life experience (not to mention knowing all the players and how to use the office equipment), I had prevailed because of my education. And yet I needed *her* help to do *my* job.

That was my intensive introduction to HR in a nutshell: A formal academic education may get you the job, but your people skills will be what helps you do the job. And keep the job.

HR professionals routinely draw a lot of fire about our preparation to be experts in a complex field. Go to any major conference and you will hear at least one academic or consultant criticize us for our assumed lack of rigor and knowledge of the ways of business. The scholars throw arcane polysyllabic vocabulary words at us as proof positive that we're utterly unprepared to lead the people function at our companies. A few consultants have chosen to make a name for themselves by haranguing us about our utter lack of imagination and creative leadership abilities. Even our leaders inside the profession have complained publicly and repeatedly about the shamefully low barriers to entry into the profession. So there's much criticism to dodge from all sides.

After more than twenty-five years in the HR world, this is what I've observed: There are many very legitimate doors into the HR profession. It's what you do with your time, energy, and passion for the field in the years you're in it that really counts. How you work your way through the complex field, what kinds of relationships you build as you go along, what kinds of results you deliver, how you help others, and how you influence the growing field—those are the things that really matter. If you ask HR people who have made it to the top role, they'll tell you that they did it through the relationships they built, the results they delivered, and the people they helped become more successful along the way. They've completed innovative projects, creating solutions to challenges that went far beyond the cookie-cutter approaches that everyone else had been using.

All the academic training in the world won't make you more inclined to approach HR in these ways if you don't have that creative, innovative personality to begin with. But, on the other hand, these successful HR careerists know that no matter how stellar their day-to-day work is, their true potential and promise depend on their passion for continuous learning.

Methods of Continuous Learning

Continuous learning is available to all of us in a variety of ways and at a variety of costs.

Independent Reading

No matter what the level at which you enter the HR profession (whether you're fresh out of school or a senior executive assigned to HR from a different management function), independent reading is a core element of your ongoing learning. You already know this, because you're reading this book. Independent reading will also help you privately fill your knowledge gaps. No one else will have to know what aspects of HR you feel weak in (or passionate about). And if you're entering the field without any basic foundation in the principles of HR at all, this is a great way to familiarize yourself with the classic theories upon which the entire profession is built. (See the recommended reading list.) Where newly arrived HR people go wrong is that they take action or make decisions intuitively because something "feels right" or "makes sense," but they don't have any knowledge to support their judgment. That knowledge is vital for double-checking the validity of decisions, and then for providing legitimizing data that will help you market your recommendations to other decision makers.

Independent reading is also available online through sites such as SHRM.org and HR.com. And you would benefit from reading *HR Magazine*, *HR Executive*, *Fortune*, *Fast Company*, and a few other leading general business publications every month. Don't forget to include in your reading list the top, most comprehensive publication serving your company's industry. It's just as important for you to understand your business as it is to stay current with your profession.

Professional Meetings

You can soak up a lot of knowledge by going to meetings that are offered either free or at low cost. Many consulting firms and law firms offer free seminars and monthly breakfasts as a way to develop their clientele. They bring in guest speakers or staffers who are content experts to deliver substantive knowledge to the people who are invited. For them it's a marketing method, so the content is bound to be great. For you it's an ongoing learning opportunity (not to mention a great networking venue).

Of course, SHRM membership (both local and national) is essential for staying current with HR and with your colleagues. SHRM has intentionally kept its membership dues low, so that they are affordable for almost everyone who is committed to advancing in an HR career—even those whose companies won't pay for their membership.

Certification Programs

Many people go for certifications for the wrong reasons. They collect them like merit badges. They want the accomplishments to put on their résumé, but they're not necessarily seeking the knowledge itself. Or they think that certification is the magic key that will unlock the otherwise sealed door to professional legitimacy. I've met more than a few certification snobs who will tell you that unless you're certified in HR, you can't really consider yourself an HR person. To be honest, I do feel that way about certain kinds of certifications. I would want to know that my pilot or my heart surgeon has the necessary certifications. But let's have just a little perspective here about the real value of certification in HR. The reason to pursue certifications in HR is your passion to pursue excellence in your field. But certification is not the only avenue to excellence, and it's a mistake to think that you're in some way inferior if you don't have PHR, SPHR, CCP, or CEBS by your name.

Likewise, when you're interviewing candidates, it's a real mistake to overlook enthusiastic, talented people who are applying for a job in your department simply because they're not certified. On the other hand, if I were considering an applicant who didn't have the right academic degree, but did have the appropriate certification, I would assume that the person had taken the initiative to learn about the field on his or her own in order to get the knowledge necessary to do the job. The fact that the candidate is certified demonstrates that he or she is taking ongoing, independent initiative to grow professionally. Candidates who have certifications have been spending their personal time—and often their personal money—seeking out this credential. That alone means a great deal.

Frankly, certification is also essential if you hope to take on a leadership role within SHRM. Most associations, in fact, take their certification process very seriously. And many won't even consider you for anything beyond entry-level volunteer jobs unless you have that credential. Thus, the career-building opportunities that participating in volunteer leadership present to you make that extra effort well worth your while.

Your Coworkers

Assuming that your company is committed to excellence in recruiting (it is, isn't it?), you have a wealth of experts right down the hall from you. The HR function has embedded in it almost every other function of an enterprise: marketing, public relations, legal, supply-chain management, research and development, even manufacturing. All your in-house experts can help you understand the sophisticated concepts and theories that inform what they do. And then you can use that insight to make the HR department all the stronger. I once had a mentor and boss with a marketing background, for instance, who taught me a great deal about how to sell what HR was doing to the senior leadership. I'm also indebted to another boss, who taught me about customer service. Her passion for customer service, both internally and externally, has changed the way I think about HR as a customer service organization for the rest of my career.

This group of experts also includes the people who work for you. This logic is easiest to understand when you hire, say, an expert compensation analyst to strengthen that area of your department. Just think how much all the generalists, including you, will learn from that person. All your coworkers can learn from one another. We all have knowledge, creativity, and expertise to bring to the conversation. Just as every organization should be a learning organization, make it also a teaching organization.

As a profession, and in our openness to receive feedback and even criticism of our abilities, we've been too tolerant of pushy, arrogant, so-called experts telling us as a group that we don't know enough to be taken seriously. It's good to be receptive to suggestions on how we can grow our careers and our shared profession, and it's important to be conversant with the basic body of HR knowledge, as well as the academic research that is available. But it's also important that we be proud of what we know, who we are, and how we're growing.

Most of us who are really serious about cultivating a solid career in HR know our stuff—at least, we know what we don't know and we know how to go about learning it. As a result, I'd love to see a collective rejection of the criticism that's heaped on us during conferences and other thought-leader gatherings.

It's not *smart* to call HR *stupid*.

No Fear:
Credibility and Confidence

CHAPTER 11

Just Because They're the Experts Doesn't Make Them More Right Than You

This is the part that always annoys management consultants—especially consultants who specialize in HR. At Southwest we confounded the experts. We did just about everything "wrong," but we still had the best performance records (on-time, customer service, baggage handling, financial) of any of the airlines. We were consistently on *Fortune's* Best Companies to Work For list, but somehow most of the trends and the fashionable HR initiatives completely eluded us. Our secret: Hire great people with great attitudes; give them a chance to succeed, grow, and build their personal future within the company; give them a unifying mission; and build a corporate culture based on integrity and respect. Period.

Once you've done that, you can start breaking all the so-called rules from the so-called experts. And you can confound their attempts to trivialize your genuine, from-the-heart corporate philosophy by condensing it into handy-dandy management tips and techniques.

Because of its performance records, Southwest had become a media and business darling. Both Harvard and Stanford did business cases on the company. Dozens of professors and management consultants from all over the country would come to see us, and they would sit down and ask many questions. Over and over again they would use the same tiresome buzzwords: TQM, reengineering, six sigma, flex hours, family-friendly—all those textbook things that had lost their meaning from overuse. No, no, no, we'd answer again and again. We didn't have those things that everyone said we were supposed to have.

They would also try to draw up some models for success. Our answer: We just hire good people. We provide a culture in which they're encouraged and motivated to continue to be good. We give them good training for their jobs, and then more good training to help them get promoted. We offer them steady career growth. And they like working here. And so they stay with us.

And they'd stare at us, saying, "You *have* to be doing this, you *have* to be following that model." We'd just shrug our shoulders. But they'd still end up writing the case studies, complete with graphs, diagrams, and models. Somehow they managed to make something that is very simple and authentic into something very complicated.

A few years ago I was asked to speak at the Institute of Management Consultants (IMC) annual meeting on what Southwest looks for when we use consultants. It was to be a relatively short and simple speech. I wrote the speech to be brutally honest with the audience: Southwest rarely uses consultants. Southwest uses consultants when (1) it doesn't have the necessary talent in house, (2) a project is so short-term that it doesn't make sense to hire permanent staff to fill the need, or (3) the company wants someone to teach it something and then go away once the staff has learned the desired skill, technique, or process. When I work with consultants, I don't want some high-handed expert coming in and telling me what to do. I want a collaborator, someone who can help us sort through our many, many ideas and select and implement the most valuable ones.

I don't want to work with someone who compares us with the other organizations in our industry and then recommends cookie-cutter approaches to diagnosed problems that may or may not exist in our company. I want someone who takes the time to understand what has made us successful and will work with us to bring about new breakthrough thinking. Someone who will help us find unique answers to our business issues.

I told the group that we wanted our consultants to be part of the team. We look for the same good attitude, work ethic, and culture match that we look for in our staff members. If consultants come in with their own agenda, they won't work with us for long. Similarly, we've worked with some consultants who were so much a part of our team that they came to our parties and even worked booths at our fund-raising events.

I have had wonderful experiences with consultants over the years. Some have helped me create unique HR initiatives tied to the business agenda. The best example of that was a large HR consulting firm that helped us formulate strategy for—and later implement—our internal branding initiative. I have also had nightmare experiences with consultants. We once hired an ergonomics consultant to evaluate the safety of our workstations. He recommended a new chair for all of our reservations agents. Luckily, before we bought thousands of expensive chairs, we found out that his family owned the chair manufacturing company. I also worked with a benefits consulting firm that recommended a plan design that made sense, but the catch was that the only administrative system that could keep track of the benefits was the system that this firm offered to its clients.

Consulting firms charge very high fees. As a rule of thumb, before I would consider using any consulting firm, I would need to be convinced that the benefits of the consulting relationship would outweigh the costs associated with the project. Will there be a cost savings or greater productivity? What will be the value added from the relationship?

As you can imagine, my comments were a shock to the IMC audience. The curmudgeons in the group said, "You can't talk to us this way! Don't you know who your audience is? Some of the behavior you described is forbidden by our code of ethics. Our members would never take advantage of client relationships." But the editor of the association newspaper asked to reprint it, and I hear it's still being used today by many consultants who want to understand what it really takes to work with a world-class client.

Consultants are good. Consultants are valuable. Consultants can bring in needed expertise just in time. But consultants aren't employees. Nor do they possess godlike wisdom. Think of consultants as saffron: The good ones are rare and very expensive. And a little goes a long way. Use them sparingly, at the right place and the right time. If you're looking for new and creative ideas, you'll be much better off brainstorming among your own group and hiring a consultant to facilitate.

Your best experts are the ones right down the hall.

CHAPTER 12

Question Authority

This chapter is going to annoy the lawyers. But some things just have to be said, the most important of which is this: Never think for a moment that your corporate attorneys have HR interests foremost in their minds when they give opinions and advice. *Your* job is to take care of HR. *Their* job is to try to keep the company out of court and its leaders out of jail. And sometimes your job and their job will conflict. If the stakes are high enough—or important enough—battling it out in a courtroom wouldn't necessarily be the worst thing in the world.

But it rarely comes to that. Usually it's just small stuff. The "safe" approach here. The "wise" approach there. Prudence rules. But HR and your people may suffer the consequences if HR always takes the safe approach and doesn't take a risk and make a stand for what's *right* now and then. Doing the right thing for your employees is often more important than protecting the company against some vague potential for trouble.

In late 2001, when anthrax was frightening mailroom workers around the country, I happened to hear a lawyer advising a group of Bay Area HR executives. Their top concern of the evening was their legal exposure in the face of terrorism. And rightly so. One of the executives said that he worked in a manufacturing facility that wasn't highly visible the way the media companies that had been hit with anthrax were. Therefore, he felt it was highly unlikely that his company would be a target for terrorism. But that day his mailroom clerks had asked if they could have latex gloves and masks to handle the mail. The low point of the presentation was when this attorney flatly and authoritatively said, "You don't have to give mailroom employees latex gloves just because they think they want them. There's no law that requires you to do this."

He may have been legally correct (although I do believe that employees have the legal right to feel safe and secure in their workplace). But he was answering the wrong question. The HR audience member had asked him whether or not to give out latex gloves to employees. The spirit behind the question was: "What steps can we take to take care of our employees legally and morally? And, if we give them the gloves, are we setting ourselves up if, God forbid, something really happened?" He wanted to protect his employer and his employees at the same time. The question the attorney was really answering was, "How do we keep ourselves from getting sued?"

This piece of advice was meant to be reassuring to the gathering. But the result may have been that all these people went back to work the next day and said to their petrified mailroom staff, "Sorry, no can do. Lawyer says no."

How much does a box of latex gloves cost? Whatever the price is in your neighborhood, it's a bargain compared with the price you pay when you lose the loyalty and respect of your employees, who want to work for a company that values their well-being—especially while on the job.

A few days later, working closely with our administrative manager, I visited our mailroom. We supplied our people with protective gear and a Plexiglas and rubber-gloved box for opening suspicious mail. We added a small premium to their hourly rate as hazardous duty pay because overnight their jobs had become different, more complex, and more difficult. It was a small cost for Yahoo!, but it meant a great deal to these employees. And it was the right thing to do.

HR is bound on all sides by rules and laws. And, yes, you certainly need to be regarded by the leadership as a trusted partner in keeping the company on the right side of legalities. However, I would like to add this: Break as many rules as you can. As long as your plans don't violate employment or labor laws, SEC or FDA rulings, or any other legal restrictions, bend and break the rules wherever you feel that a fundamental HR value or principle is at stake. If your HR principle is to make sure that your employees can feel reasonably secure while they're handling miscellaneous envelopes, *buy the box of latex gloves, already!*

Develop the habit of questioning authority of all kinds. And you might as well start with your employment lawyers. Remember, their job is to protect you from lawsuits, not to support you while you create a dynamic, alive HR function. There will always be people who will tell you that you can't or shouldn't do something. If you're not equipped with a prestigious law degree, you might think it's prudent to believe them. You might, for instance, believe the attorney who tells you that it's illegal to hire for anything other than skills. That's not true at all. It's illegal to discriminate against people because of their age (if they're over forty), race, nationality, and so on. And somewhere along the line, attorneys found that a useful rule of thumb is to emphasize performance, experience, and skills. By training HR to look only at those attributes, the legal department can protect recruiters from violating truly meaningful civil rights laws. But there is no civil rights law that gathers jerks and misfits into a protected class. Still, we hire jerks and misfits because attorneys tell us we can look only for performance, experience, and skills.

In human resources, we have far more creative leeway in the way we run our operations than we're in the habit of exploring. There usually is a far better way of doing something than the established rules would have us believe. It will probably come as no surprise that I learned this lesson very well at Southwest. Herb Kelleher made it his personal mission not to do anything by the book, and he is a lawyer. And I saw firsthand—especially in the compensation arena—how his maverick style opened up the potential for truly spectacular results.

When I first beheld the Southwest compensation plan, I couldn't believe my eyes. I noticed that many non-airline-specific jobs were paying 20 percent or even more below the market rate. I wondered, "Why would these people want to work here?" According to the "official rules" I had learned in an American Compensation Association (now WorldatWork) certification course, if an employer is below the 15 percent differential, it is in serious jeopardy of losing its talent. That was the *rule*. But here I saw a value override the rule: the value of the intangibles that made working at Southwest so attractive that the company could defy the accepted way of doing things. Employees were saying through their commitment (even at lower pay), "I love my job, I love my coworkers, I love what I'm doing. I'm willing to make less because I see the future in this company." Those employees could have done 20 percent better somewhere else, but guess what? They could also have been laid off after September 11, as hundreds of thousands of their counterparts at other airlines were. At Southwest, they weren't.

A Lobster Is Not a Dog

Strict overemphasis on rules can also discourage employees from thinking independently and making the best decisions for their customers. Even at relatively freewheeling companies like Southwest, employees may take certain rules and regulations to extremes. One of Southwest's most rigid rules, for instance, is that it does not carry live animals (except for service animals, such as guide dogs and search-and-rescue dogs). The airline's business model depends on twenty-minute turnarounds at the gate, and that poses too much of a danger to animals, who require safe, careful, and therefore slow handling. The airline is full of pet-loving employees, and no one wants to face the prospect of a passenger's pet being lost—or worse—in transit. This rule is an easy one to enforce. And it's so cut and dried that who would have thought it was subject to original thinking? Until one day . . .

If you've ever flown out of any of the coastal New England cities, you're familiar with those shops selling live lobsters in cardboard cartons. Animal. Live. No live animals. Right? That's what our gate agent concluded when someone wanted to check his lobster: No lobsters allowed. The hapless passenger had to leave his dinner behind!

We didn't fire the gate agent for being so rigidly attached to the rules. But the airline has been using this story ever since as an illustration of how common sense can tell you to break the rules.

Can you teach people good judgment? Probably not. Once they're adults, they pretty much have their judgment skills in place. But what you can do is cultivate a workplace culture in which it's safe to use *independent* judgment. Start with yourself and then extend the principle throughout the organization, especially to your customer service representatives. They're your link to your buying public.

And the next time you observe a lawyer rigidly sticking to a stupid rule (as opposed to a law—let's be clear about that), send him or her a lobster dinner and a copy of this book with this chapter explicitly marked.

CHAPTER 13

Start Your Own Hole-in-the-Wall Gang

This is a paradox, but it's true. You're in one of the most people-oriented professions in corporate life. And the higher up you go in the ranks, the more famous you are inside the organization. You are probably known by more employees than any other leader inside the company, with the possible exception of the CEO. A lot of people know your name, and, if you practice HR from the heart, my bet is that you know a lot of people by their names.

But it's also true that yours is probably one of the more isolated professions in your company. The higher up you go, the less people know and understand what it is that you do, the secrets you keep, and the decisions you have to make. You can't always bounce your ideas off someone else in the company, even if you speak in the most general terms, because your colleagues might guess whom you're talking about. You can't necessarily discuss your concerns with your spouse or partner. He or she might not be able to grasp the whole picture. (Or, if your spouse is like my husband, he or she will usually take your side, and occasionally you might actually be wrong.) You need a community of peers who know exactly what you're dealing with and what the issues are, and who can maybe even offer some solutions based on their experiences. Who you gonna call? Personally, I'm fond of my Hole-in-the-Wall Gang.

Over the years I have had the privilege of being associated with some of the most dynamic and exciting official groups in human resources management: the Society for Human Resource Management (and its predecessor, the American Society for Personnel Administration) and its various levels of participation, especially the national, Dallas, and student chapters; the American Compensation Association (now WorldatWork); and the Dallas Business Group on Health. I have regularly attended groups of very senior HR leaders in both Dallas and Silicon Valley. But my favorite group was a personal just-folks clutch of HR peers in Dallas that we called the Hole-in-the-Wall Gang.

We only had one governing rule, and it was a fun one: We could meet and eat only at holes in the wall. (But we did have official bylaws, which appear later in this chapter.) We met once a month in some of Dallas's most colorful dives and had some of the best food: tamales, tacos, chicken-fried steak, fried oysters. These were HR folks from all over Greater Dallas. But during these monthly meetings, we were there just to laugh and laugh. It was a great stress reliever. But more than that, we were cementing solid relationships of trust and sharing. If one of us was facing an HR issue that we didn't know what to do about, we'd throw it out to the group and let the group gnaw on the issue as we were gnawing on a barbecue bone.

In another, more formal senior group, an outsider might think that we'd be in danger of sharing competitive information with one another. After all, the top HR guy from American Airlines was right there with me, the top HR person from Southwest Airlines. But I never worried about sharing what I was doing with this group. I could have handed over the entire blueprint of Southwest's HR strategy to these people, and even if they tried to adopt it, it wouldn't be the same. Every company was so different in culture (even American Airlines) that we could freely share with one another and not worry about losing our competitive edge. We knew that we wouldn't be able to successfully steal information—even if we wanted to, which we didn't—because what worked for one company simply couldn't be directly applied to the next. But we could certainly help one another figure out how to deal with our issues.

There are no rules for starting a Hole-in-the-Wall Gang. Simply pick up the phone, call your counterparts, and get together for lunch. Make sure the restaurant is a fun, no pretense joint, and you'll quickly get out of business mode and just enjoy being yourself with some of the few people in town who can really understand.

Hole-in-the-Wall Lunch Gang Official By-Laws

No knives or forks allowed.
(at least with BBQ ribs)

No straws allowed.
(sissies and city folks use straws)

Eating with hat or cap on is encouraged.

Use of toothpick acceptable.
(sign of being economical in getting all the food ya paid for)

Only longneck drinks (soda and beer) permitted.

Belching is allowed.
(sign of satisfaction with the food one has consumed)

Talking with food in your mouth is ok.

Limited amount of HR discussion allowed.
(don't want anyone to lose their taste for the good food)

Must attend regularly.
(don't let other things that might seem more important interfere—friendship is more important)

Developed and promulgated by Larry Burk, SPHR, CCP, Compensation Manager of the Boy Scouts of America, and Jim Wilkins, SPHR, retired SHRM Area IV Manager.

No Fear:
Credibility and Confidence

CHAPTER 14

The Dais of Our Lives

We have many things to worry about these days: working in high-rise buildings, corporate corruption, the stock market, keeping our jobs, getting through airport security quickly enough to make our flights, the oddly friendly guy next door. Still, I'm amazed to say, the phobia that's top on our worry list remains the same: public speaking. It's not too hard to understand why: It takes enormous courage, arrogance, or ego to think that what we have to say is so important that a roomful of people should give up their lunch hour or dinner with their families to hear the golden gems as they drop from our lips. And, quite frankly, most of us weren't raised to think of ourselves in that grandiose way.

Here's an invitation to look at it in a different way. HR by its very nature is a dynamic, living, ever-changing profession. Somewhere in the HR world, we know something new today that we didn't know yesterday. That's the way it is with a profession that specializes in people. And if you're an observant, engaged HR practitioner who is aware of the changes and the things that have been learned in your own company, you are as much an expert and a pioneer in some aspect of your field as the highest-paid so-called thought leader. You've got something to share with the rest of us. It's almost your professional, civic duty to do exactly that. And the best way to deliver that information (and often the fastest) is through public speaking.

It's also great for both your career and your company. Public speaking grows on itself: The more you speak, the more you learn as you prepare for a presentation and the more you're considered an expert in that topic; the more you're considered an expert, the more in demand you will be; the more in demand you are, the more desirable you will be to employers (including your own) and headhunters. (And if you think you might someday be a consultant, you would be really smart to get over any fears of public speaking now. Consultants depend on speaking for both building business and generating income.) Your company benefits in that the more you're out there telling good stories about how it does business, the better its reputation will be among all its constituencies: customers, competitors, employees, future employees, shareholders, vendors, academics looking for case studies of excellence, and so on.

Speaking comes easily to most of us—until we are standing up in front of more people than we can count on our fingers. Everyone has a different comfort level beyond which a relaxed conversation turns into a full-blown presentation with full-blown jitters, with terribly important things at stake. In my case, it took only one person to transform me from a moderately confident student speaker into a ball of nerves, giving me a legacy of anxiety that I took with me well into my young professional life. You just never know when the heebie-jeebies are going to get you!

I had a promising—if rather ordinary—start. Growing up in southern Louisiana, I had plenty of opportunities to get up in front of audiences. I was in the choir at church and sang some solos in my high school choir. My voice quivered, my lips quivered, and you couldn't hear a sound come out of my mouth. But that choir director, bless his heart, kept making me get up again and again. And I got used to it. I was also in my school's drama department, wrestling with my nerves. But there I had a technique: I got into character as soon as I could. I'm not Libby, I'm this character, and there's no way she'd be nervous up there just being herself. And it worked.

So by the time I was in college taking an undergraduate speech class, I had a good grounding in standing up in front of a group, opening my mouth, and making something intelligible come out. But still, every time I stood up in front of the class, I was absolutely horrible. I knew it, the teacher knew it, and, I'm afraid, the entire class suspected it. Then one day, which I will never ever forget, the class knew it for sure.

I was assigned to give a speech on the war in Lebanon, and I had prepared that thing to a fare-thee-well. I had done my homework; I had the statistics and the details; I even had visual aids. I was *ready*. So I walked to the front of the room, set up my materials, turned around to address the class, and spotted *him*! A friend of mine was sitting in the back of the room wearing a T-shirt with a tuxedo printed on the front. For some reason, right then and there I started laughing. And I laughed. And laughed. And laughed. For what seemed like fifteen straight minutes, I just laughed.

Well, that did it. It was firmly planted in my mind that any time I stood up to speak, I would break down into gales of laughter. How could I even risk it? As anyone who has struggled to keep a straight face during a somber occasion knows, nothing will throw you into fits of giggles as quickly as worrying that you'll laugh at precisely the worst possible moment.

But I was destined to live the speaking life. Right away with my first job I was assigned to give new hires their orientation. So, like it or not, I was speaking. Fortunately for me, my new job coincided with a new marriage to David Sartain, who is a brilliant speaker—among his many gifts. He steered me to Toastmasters. I even helped start a Toastmasters chapter at my office. Always looking for the fun in challenges, I started participating in official Toastmasters contests. And I discovered the fun and joy of sharing what I know with other people in an entertaining way. My work to address my fear became a crucial aspect of my professional life, opening important doors for me both in my career and as I rose through the volunteer ranks at SHRM. Most of all, the ability to speak in public forums (as well as my blossoming enthusiasm for it) has allowed me to make a difference in the national conversation about what it means to be a progressive, productive, and profitable employer.

With the help of my friends at Toastmasters, and later a Dale Carnegie course, I was able to get over my fear of speaking and take my HR messages to a lot of other places, from local Rotary Club meetings in Dallas to SHRM chapter meetings to conference general sessions, and even all the way to Congress, where I testified on behalf of my profession before the Senate Committee on Families and Children. My speaking life has taken me all over the country, and I have even been invited to speak in such exotic locations as Turkey and Mexico City. It has positioned me as an expert in my field in the eyes of not only my audiences but also my employees and my bosses, and it has given me the extraordinary opportunity to represent private industry's best intentions and perspectives in a moment of American history. That's not a bad trade-off for getting a grip on the giggles, I'd say.

Less Is More . . . When You Give 'Em What They Need

A couple of years after the passage of the Family and Medical Leave Act (FMLA), I was invited by SHRM to speak on a panel with two women who had helped to write and pass the FMLA. Each of us had been asked to prepare a ten-minute summary of our evaluation of the act, how it was performing relative to what it had been intended to do, and what the real-life implications of administering the act in the workplace were. My carefully prepared presentation discussed how difficult it had been for Southwest to administer the law consistently for 25,000 people (at the time), the complexity of the law, the difficulty of merging the requirements of the law with our already generous benefits and leave programs, and how the one-size-fits-all approach didn't work for us. I was prepared to talk about how the government's definition of a "serious health condition" allowed just about any infirmity as a reason for a leave and how the intermittent leave provisions made it difficult to plan for staffing. I was prepared to tell personal stories of rising employee absences, unnecessary administrative burdens, and increased operational problems. I had all this great stuff to share. But I never got the chance.

Each of my co-panelists spoke for more than twenty minutes! It was a fifty-minute session, and so there were only ten minutes left. By this time, the auditorium was filled with three hundred angry HR professionals who wanted to eat these two panelists alive. They didn't get to hear from their colleague and representative (me), and they were in some real danger of missing their precious Q&A opportunity. I had to think fast. What was the right approach? I jettisoned all my wonderful material and cobbled together in my head a two-minute statement, with the idea of sacrificing at least eight minutes to give them a chance to ask their questions.

So here was my opening remark: "I don't know about you folks, but I must have been living on a different planet from these two ladies for the last three years." The crowd went wild. I got a standing ovation. (And that took up at least a minute of my remaining two minutes.) Then I said, "If I had more time, I would tell you about what it's like to comply with the FMLA while running a 25,000-employee airline that already has generous health and leave plans. And then I would tell you that I, like these other two women, am a mother. I went into labor at work. I then had my daughter in day care. I have personally faced in my own real life every issue they brought up as hypotheticals. But since these ladies didn't leave me any time to speak, let me open it up to you for questions." Back on their feet, the audience used up even more of their Q&A time applauding my brief comments.

Less is better. I proved my point with few words. The headline of the next issue of *HR News* gave my few comments more space than the others' presentations, and the more than 100,000 SHRM members who weren't at the conference received the information they needed—minus the spin from the political wonks.

What Will You Speak About?

In the twenty-five years that I've been attending business gatherings of all sizes, I've come to the conclusion that there are two kinds of speakers: those who are in it because of their passion for their topic and those who are in it because of their passion for the speaker's fee—

and if you've ever paid for a speaker, you know that we're talking big bucks here. I'm certainly not implying that great speakers shouldn't be paid well. But most of us can tell which speakers are talking from their hearts and which are talking from their profit motive.

The first part of the giveaway is their subject matter and how intimate they are with their topic. Open up any speakers' directory and you'll see the same subjects listed so often that your eyes will cross: motivation, successful selling, team building, change management, leadership, and any number of animals used as the metaphor of the moment—moose, elephants, fish, and mice, to name a few. Those who are professional speakers first (as opposed to genuine experts) had once asked themselves what they would speak about and had picked the "hot" topics. And that's why you see these topics listed again and again.

You are already an expert on something. Even if you're just starting out in the field, you're an expert on how to take your education and parlay it into a promising early career. Are you a key player in a company initiative that's so original that it sets your company apart from the rest of your community? Speak about that. Are you passionate about your company's diversity program? Speak about that. Do you believe that HR should be listed as one of the Top 10 Hot Careers of the Decade? Great! Do you think that HR as a profession should just wise up and get real? What's holding you back? (Audiences love provocateurs, as long as they know that, in your heart, you're on their side and as long as you have an airtight case supporting your main points.) There's even plenty of room for more insight, inspiration, and information on change management, leadership, and team building. Just be sure that what you have to offer is content drawn from your *own* insights and observations.

Jane Austen's famous advice to writers holds true for speakers as well: Start with what you know best. From that point you can branch out. And the speaking side of your working life will take you in directions beyond your wildest dreams.

CHAPTER 15

Can This Marriage Be Saved?

It happens every time. I am in a room full of HR professionals. I am sharing my vision, talking about culture or internal branding or becoming an employer of choice, and suddenly a hand shoots up, sometimes timidly. "What if my CEO doesn't support my initiatives?" "What if my CEO doesn't understand or care about HR?" Presumably the HR professionals in my audience had carefully considered their CEOs' interest in HR and its mission before agreeing to work for the company. How could they have been snookered so badly that they're now asking me these questions in a public forum?

CEOs aren't stupid. If they want you to agree to head up their HR department, they know all the right things to do and say in order to court you and win you over. You'll hear a lot about core values, "most important assets," mission, desire to change the world, internal stakeholders, and vision. In this day and age, I guarantee you, you will never hear a CEO say, "Just do the bare minimum to keep them out of my hair and me out of jail."

But that doesn't mean that some aren't thinking just that. Most CEOs don't really understand the value HR can bring to their organization. They can't help it. Believe it or not, HR isn't the most important thing they deal with on a daily basis. But, if you ask them, most of them will tell you that they spend most of their time on "people issues."

Did you hear that? The key to your success in this situation is to remember that CEOs typically don't get all that excited about HR itself. That's not their job; that's *your* job. But they do worry about talent. Do they have the right mix? Is a new team member a bad fit? What should be done about it? Two top executives don't see eye to eye. Or the entire team at the top isn't in a high-performance mode. Is the organization or its leaders capable of moving to the next level? Can we implement the strategy? No, CEOs don't get that excited about HR. But they can get excited about what HR can do for them. Very few CEOs wake up in the morning and say, "Hot dog! I've got a great new compensation and benefits plan!" But they may get worked up about what an incredible company of world-class talent they're running and how that talent is helping them exceed Wall Street's expectations quarter after quarter. Now, that's exciting stuff! And, conversely, if the organization is losing its best people, you can be sure that HR will be charged with fixing the problem, pronto.

As we've already discussed, if you are considering moving to a new company, you have the chance to do your homework and to determine whether or not all is as it seems. If it's not, you'll be able to dodge the bullet and turn down the job offer. But every once in a while topnotch, savvy HR candidates get nailed by sweet-talking executives in the recruiting mode. And before long, they find that they are caught inside a company that is absolutely resistant to any of their ideas, initiatives, and values. And that's because the CEO is resistant. Perhaps they misread the perceived sincerity of the CEO's words during the interview phase. Or perhaps changing business conditions and economic pressures have changed the CEO's priorities. Or perhaps their excellent CEO left and was replaced by a not-so-excellent CEO. Or perhaps they went in with their eyes wide open, thinking that they had what it takes to change the organization for the better, and now they find out that they are out-muscled. They are working for a CEO who doesn't respect HR. If that happens to you, at least there's some comfort in knowing that you're not alone in having this problem.

Sure, you can resign. But you can *always* resign. There's plenty of time for that. So before you do, why not try a little exercise? The results may not save the company from the CEO, and they may not save your position there. But the experience may strengthen your business acumen. And who knows? If you do end up leaving, maybe you will have prepared the ground so that your replacement will have a better experience.

Here's the exercise: Find out what keeps your company's leaders up at night worrying. What are their key burning issues? Ask them directly. Ask the executive assistant. Ask the leadership team. Read the CEO's speeches and open letters from the last twelve months. Read the business plan. Read the latest annual report. Find out what is important to the CEO and understand the industry. Listen carefully to the CEO's vocabulary, noting the most frequently used key words.

Okay, suppose you still don't have a clue as to what is important. Make a few assumptions. Every CEO of a public company should be interested in return on investment. If your company isn't publicly traded, who are its stakeholders? (You can convince the CEO that the employees are stakeholders later.) Customers and investors are important, as well as brand leadership and building market share. What demographic trends will affect your company's future success? Is your company global? Does it need to be? What is going on in your industry? How is your company positioned against the competition? Is it seeking to acquire other businesses, or might it be acquired? Is government regulation or deregulation looming in the future? What technological advances will affect your organization's future? Can these put the company out of business or help it to create value?

And then ask yourself and your HR leadership team: How can the people side of the business help the company address those issues? What is your organizational strategy? What capabilities do you need as an organization to execute the strategy? Focus on what the CEO needs, not on what you can deliver or solve. Can you supply what is needed? What can you do that is creative and innovative, and not just another HR tool out of the proverbial tool kit or a flavor-of-the-month management fad?

When your turn comes to discuss the value of HR, speak in terms of those issues, not just the HR efforts you put into place to deal with them. Stop using the language of HR. What CEO can get excited about employee records, the handbook, the policies, the discipline and termination process, the interviewing process, the new hire orientation, the performance evaluation form, or the latest merit increase program? Instead, formulate an HR agenda that delivers results that are aligned with the CEO's agenda. Address the most important goals of the company. Talk about the people as individuals. Use real data (numbers and measurements), but don't forget to mention the intangible aspects of what you deliver. Leaders who are tone-deaf to all the marvels that are HR won't be tone-deaf to your HR *contributions* when you can speak in terms of their desired outcomes. Then they'll hear you loud and clear! This is your chance to rebrand the HR department as a valuable resource to your company.

At Southwest, for instance, we found that becoming "the People Department" was a crucial first step. It was downright ironic: Here was a company that truly believed that people created its sustainable competitive advantage, that intangibles were as important as tangibles in creating return on investment, that having the best talent was a competitive strategy. But HR *as a function* was not seen as the owner or even the driver of these results, and the organization didn't value HR as either a function or a profession. Over the years, several incredibly sharp, well-intentioned HR leaders had tried their best to demonstrate the value that HR provides. Each new leader added to the HR agenda, to the business success, to the employee experience, to the culture, to the DNA that made Southwest legendary. Sadly, HR was still not fully appreciated for its value-added.

Anything that felt like a typical "HR program" just didn't work in that culture. It was too bureaucratic. So our challenge was to go about the business of HR in a new way. There were many meetings in which we on the HR team sat in the room and asked ourselves, "So how do we make this look like a way of life at Southwest instead of an HR program?" In other words, how do we hide the peas under the mashed potatoes? Everything we did had to be simple. It had to be focused on people. It had to be unique. And it had to be a way of life rather than an HR initiative. We had to involve other departments. Our best-practice employment process worked because it was a partnership with line management. Our University for People was successful because we worked closely with our operational areas to identify what they needed in front-line leaders. And then we designed and delivered what they needed, not what we wanted to offer. Our highly valued benefits program worked because we made it fun, we kept it fresh, and we communicated the outcomes of the program constantly. What we did *enhanced* our culture, but we didn't try to redefine it.

Even if you can make the HR program palatable to your company, you most likely can't get everything done at once. So start by building a fan base. Pick wins and fill some needs. Find something that everyone is complaining about and make improvements. Do something that saves money. When I joined Southwest, I quickly determined that the organization wasn't ready for some of the creative compensation plans I had implemented at previous companies. Rather than being frustrated, my team and I designed and implemented creative benefit programs that provided significant cost savings to the company while offering a more valuable benefit to our people. Once I had demonstrated my capability in this area, I had the opportunity to present some more creative ideas about compensation.

It is very difficult to get support and buy-in from the senior executives if the basic HR services aren't executed flawlessly. We invite disrespect when we overpromise and underdeliver. The best way to get respect is to deliver what you promise. Just try to sell an innovative employee incentive plan when last year's bonus checks weren't sent out on time. Try to implement a leadership development program when the last one was boring or ineffective. Before embarking on your grand strategy, audit your processes and be sure your internal customers are happy with your current services. Set realistic expectations and develop ways to measure your accomplishments. That will show the entire organization that HR does provide tangible results.

If you can't get support from everyone, find one willing partner for a new initiative. Let's say the head of customer service is ready to implement new processes to develop leadership bench strength in her organization. Now you have an opportunity to show what you can do.

Together you identify the long-term need for leadership talent and the future competencies needed. You design a comprehensive process that combines the best of performance management, leadership development, and career management to groom existing star employees for future leadership roles. Now suddenly other departments will be asking why you haven't offered that program to their group. Over time, you will have made a real difference.

There is another way in which CEOs demonstrate that they don't respect HR that is just the opposite of what you might suppose: They expect *too much* from HR. Sometimes they expect us to be miracle workers. Is there a perceived retention problem? The CEO instructs you to design a new compensation plan. The problem is that in fact it's a *leadership* problem, not a compensation problem. The leaders aren't effective? "Then put in a new training program," the CEO says. But that won't work without great senior leaders and the right support from the very top.

In our enthusiasm to promote the HR function, we run the risk of overmarketing ourselves. Be a leader. Drive the HR agenda, but learn when to say no. Teach your CEO what is realistic to expect from HR. And when your leaders finally understand exactly what HR does for business, they will appreciate your contribution to the company's long-term objectives. And then you'll get the lasting respect that HR deserves and that it needs if it is to be even more effective in its partnership with the company's strategic team.

CHAPTER 16

How to Know When It's Time to Leave

When you build your HR career and your HR department from the heart, you will enjoy many emotionally rewarding results. Every day you'll see the direct results of your vision, creativity, and patience. You will have the immense satisfaction of working in a smart, productive, and emotionally healthy organization that directly reflects the values that you have put into action over time. The company culture will reflect that one-big-happy-family ideal—or at least it will come very close to it. You may actually have achieved some fame locally, nationally, or even globally for your accomplishments. After investing many years in creating this fabulous, self-perpetuating community, you can finally sit back and enjoy the results.

Don't do it. At least, don't do it for very long. Today's success currency isn't about what you've achieved in the past, it's about your capacity to learn and grow in the immediate future. And if you think you've done all you can in your current company, I hate to be the one to tell you this: It's probably time to move on. For when you build your HR career and your HR department from the heart, you will also put yourself at risk for serious career-growth hazards. Those emotional rewards can become emotional entanglements. You can become so personally identified with one company that no one—not even you—can picture you thriving anywhere else. You've stopped learning. You're merely recycling the initiatives of previous years. Maybe it's time for you to move along.

Leaving Southwest was like getting a divorce—it was horribly wrenching. I was so personally involved with many of the employees there. It was such a joy to see the employees' children who were born when I first started there begin junior high. I was even starting to go to the weddings of children who had been young when I started. Southwest's HR department was also making great progress. We had made *Fortune*'s 100 Best Companies to Work For list for four years in a row, and we were well on our way to the fifth year's list. While everyone else in the country was complaining about the war for talent and labor shortages, we were receiving over 10,000 résumés a month. We were attracting spirited employees who expected to love their work at Southwest. And we made good on that expectation. As a result, Southwest was known as much for its people as for its outstanding on-time and baggage-handling records. And I was traveling around the country helping other HR practitioners understand what it means to run their departments *from the heart*. I was building my personal brand.

It was a great time to be at Southwest. So, it was time to leave. In fact, I probably should have left a couple of years earlier.

Here's the typical HR one-job lifespan: It takes you three years to get a job exactly where you want it. Year One is the time you need to figure things out, build relationships, evaluate the staff, understand the culture, figure out the power system, learn the business, and identify whom to keep and whom to help move on. By the time you reach Year Two, you're ready to set the agenda and put all the players in place to make the big changes that you've designed to help the company grow. By Year Three, you're enjoying your accomplishments, tweaking the results here and there, and designing new initiatives.

This is when you should ask yourself The Question: Have I done everything? Or is there still more to do and to learn? Ideally, you can find a company where you can cycle through Years Two and Three again and again, growing as you help your company grow. That's what happened for me at Southwest. But if you're not growing and learning every year, and if there is no prospect for additional progress in the future, it's time to get the word out to the headhunters that you're receptive to their phone calls.

How do you know where you are in this job life cycle? Write a new résumé every year. Every January, while other people are writing their resolutions, I'm reviewing the past year. What were my significant accomplishments in the past twelve months? What were your top significant achievements last year? Make a regular practice of writing them down as the year comes to a close. If you don't have anything new to put on your updated résumé, it's probably time to leave. If you don't have any new projects on the horizon, it's probably time to leave. If you are there only because you love the people you work with and have been named godparent of fifteen of their newborns, record their addresses, phone numbers, and e-mail addresses and promise that you'll write.

The Five Best Reasons for Staying Put

1. *You are working on an innovative, strategic project that will change the organization.* And you want to finish it and see the results. For me this was Southwest's internal branding initiative, which was completed in 2000. These kinds of opportunities are few and far between.

2. *Personal reasons.* Perhaps your child is a senior in high school, and you don't want to spoil his or her last year by changing jobs or locations. Maybe one of your parents is ill, and you need to focus on helping out during this time. Or maybe you have a child with learning disabilities who is doing very well in his or her current learning environment. If you are happy enough in your work not to disrupt your personal life, then sometimes your personal priorities prevail.

3. *You're in line for a promotion to a great opportunity.* You see the very real possibility that your dream job within the company may be within reach.

4. *You are gaining new skills or expertise that you need before you move on.* Let's say you are implementing a sales commission plan, or redesigning benefits, or implementing succession planning, or creating a groundbreaking leadership development program. Having this on your résumé will help you land the next job.

5. *You are developing a successor, and that person needs just a little more seasoning.* If you really want to see what you have created endure into the future, be sure you have one or two groomed successors who can follow in your footsteps. Someone who was trained by you will perpetuate what the team has created and even make it better by adding her or his special touches.

The Five Best Reasons for Leaving

1. *You are not having fun anymore.* You used to wake up raring to go, full of energy. But now each week seems more like work than it used to. Evaluate and understand why this is happening. If you find very real reasons that can't be changed, then polish up your résumé.

2. *Things won't change for the better.* You have tried to change the important elements of the organization that you feel must change; you have taken responsibility for making things better. If repeated efforts to solve the problem have failed, you face a choice: Stay where conditions will continue to bother you, or find a different environment.

3. *Your organization has stopped learning and growing.* If you are not *ahead* of your competitors, they will quickly gain on you. If your organization is not learning faster and growing faster, the

downward spiral is about to begin. If you are the only one who is trying to make improvements happen, and you can't convince others that change is needed, go where your ideas are welcome.

4. *There's no way for you to move up.* Is your successor ready to step up, yet there is no next step for you? Maybe your next step is to go elsewhere. If you stay, you probably will not be learning or growing, and you are keeping someone else from the next step.

5. *You run out of silver bullets.* You are so often the messenger who brings the bad news, you are so often asking the really tough questions, and you are so often disturbing the equilibrium that eventually you wear out your welcome. A good friend of mine who runs a very successful outplacement business once told me that he thought HR executives have only so many silver bullets. You know you've run out of silver bullets when your senior leadership team stops listening to your great ideas and powerful solutions. They roll their eyes and humor you, but you no longer have the ability to be the change agent you must be. You're feeling uneasy and ineffective. Take a look at your feet. That's where you'll find that last bullet lodged.

Buh-bye.

CHAPTER 17

How to Get a Job That Is Far Better Than the One You Wanted

Have faith that something even better is waiting for you. I know, that's easier said than done, especially when the stakes are high, your mortgage payment is due, and your kids are college-bound. But I know you'll agree with me on these two points: Even though we spend our careers hiring others, we HR professionals are just as nervous and lost as the next person when it comes to job hunting. And, any time you go looking for a job, you're going to get discouraged more than you're going to be encouraged.

You may be a pro at résumé writing and at counseling others on the fine points of job interviewing. But when it's *your* career (not to mention your food, shelter, and credit rating) that's on the line, you're just as exposed and vulnerable as everyone else. You have to be prepared for rejection and be ready to take it on the chin without taking it personally—which, you and I both know, it is. When you don't get the job (or even the interview), the company is saying, "We've had the chance to take a good look at you, and you know what? We don't want you." Ouch. What could be more personal than that?

But just as you would reassure someone else: You don't know the whole picture at that company. You're on the outside looking at a carefully constructed facade of perfection. But, just as you know different about your company, the people at that company know different about theirs. And even though you see what appears to be a perfect match, what they see is someone who doesn't fit the culture or the objectives they're trying to achieve through HR. Or worse: They don't know what they want at all. Or perhaps even worse: They know what they *should* want, and they know that you're just the person who could make it happen for them. They say all the right things in the interview. You say all the right things in the interview. It looks like the perfect values match. You're dead sure you will get the offer. You leave on cloud nine. Then . . . nothing. As much as they may want it intellectually, the change you represent is more than they can emotionally handle, and they run screaming. It's like the guy who says, "I'll call you," at the end of a perfect date. Yeah, right.

Over the years I received plenty of inquiries from headhunters. And I was just too happy at Southwest to even consider changing jobs. So I would politely send them on their way, with a few names and numbers of other job seekers that they might want to investigate. But finally, late in 2000, after much discussion with my family, I decided that the time had come to investigate new opportunities. And I resolved that I would listen to the next search firm that called me.

When I first decided to start looking for a new job after thirteen years at Southwest, I did everything that most job seekers should do. I started making plans secretly. I began to let it be known among the better headhunters that I would listen to possibilities, and I started working with a coach to refine my interviewing skills and rewrite my résumé. (That's right. I was going to be interviewing at a higher level than ever before—with the CEO—so I needed to upgrade my own packaging. I needed help, and I knew it. So I got it.)

On January 3, 2001, after the big decision, I received a call from a headhunter who sent me to Silicon Valley, where I met the CEO of an exciting—and *secure*—Internet-based company. The interview went well. I was invited back for a second day to interview with what seemed like the entire leadership team. At the end of the day, the CEO told me, "I'm going to offer you the job. I'll have a package for you on Friday. And I'd like you, your husband, and your daughter to come out and spend the weekend with my family."

So I flew back to Dallas with a big potential secret in my heart. That Thursday I was scheduled for my monthly meeting with my boss. I didn't want to spend half a day with her on Thursday, only to officially resign on Friday. That just didn't seem honest. So I took the risk and gave her the news. I told her I wasn't certain I'd get the offer but it looked as though I would.

So the cat was out of the bag. I was as good as gone. My boss knew that I was prepared to say yes, but made no attempt to start a discussion about a counter-offer. (In fact, she agreed it was time for me to leave.) So we finished the meeting, and I looked forward to hearing from the California company on Friday. I was certain I would. 9 A.M., no offer. 11 A.M., no offer. 2:30 P.M., no offer. 4 P.M., no offer. 4:30 P.M., no offer. 4:45 P.M., no offer. 5 P.M., no offer. *No offer!*

So there I was, officially leaving Southwest Airlines with no place to go. Now I was committed. I was definitely leaving. Through the entire process that followed, I defined for myself what kind of company I was most interested in. The more companies I looked at in the interview process, the more I came to understand what my next best step would be. And I discovered that two characteristics most attracted me. My preferred candidate company would be in an early stage, but way past start-up, heading for the exciting growth stage. But it would also have to be clearly destined to "make it," so that all it needed was time. Alternatively, the company would have a new CEO who was building a whole new leadership team and needed to change the company's culture and business direction.

And so I invested several months interviewing with many companies that were household names—and either rejecting or being rejected by a string of them. At one company, I knew that there had been a rapid turnover of a series of HR leaders. Once again the job was open. There were synergies between that organization and Southwest. I met with the president and CEO, and he said all the right things. So I presented the chairman with a sort of ultimatum: "Don't hire me unless you're prepared to do this, this, this, this, and this." My message to that company was, "If you don't want HR to have a seat at the table and have significant impact, if you don't want to keep working on the corporate culture, save us both valuable time." The company didn't waste my time. Later I heard that the person who was hired left after three months. The company didn't support proposed HR initiatives.

A major nonprofit organization, one that I supported and believed in, on the other hand, told me flat out, "We don't want you because our culture is more serious than what you're used to." That's probably true. Anyway, it was also for the best. Toward the end of 2001, the organization's president and CEO resigned in a huge dispute with the board, and I would have been in the middle of that.

I went to the East Coast to interview with a major retail chain. I loved the CEO. He was doing a turnaround. A new leadership team had been hired. The ambiance in the stores was going to be new, different, and appealing to the chain's customers. I was disappointed when the company selected another candidate.

The hardest choice involved one of the two airlines that reached out to me. A major airline in my city offered me a wonderful job. It wanted HR to drive many cultural changes and to engage its people. It would have been a natural transition for me, and I thought very highly of the airline's leadership team. But I wanted a change. In fact, the one place I *didn't* want to work was the airline industry. If I had accepted its offer, I would have joined it the Tuesday after Labor Day 2001. I would have been on the job precisely one week before all hell broke loose. And I can only assume that with the devastating turn of events, HR initiatives had to be put on the back burner.

A few months after my Silicon Valley disappointment, I hosted a reception at the SHRM annual conference in San Francisco. A consultant from Hewitt approached me and said, "I hear you're leaving Southwest." I confirmed it and told him what I was looking for. His eyes widened, and he said, "Oh my gosh! I know just the company!" Yahoo!, he said, was losing the head of HR, who was taking a sabbatical but most likely would not be returning, and the head of compensation and benefits had left at the same time. Yahoo! had both the criteria that I was looking for—a young but established company with great promise, strong brand, *and* a changing leadership. And here all this time I had been thinking that I'd have to settle for either/or.

When it's right, it's right. And it usually happens pretty quickly. I had the job offer three weeks later. All it took was twenty-four years, hundreds of hours of interviewing and résumé writing, and one cocktail party overlooking the twinkling hills of nighttime San Francisco.

The key to finding the next opportunity that will make you happy is finding the position that is perfect for both you *and* the hiring company. The company must want you as badly as you want it. When you find that situation, you've got the match of your dreams.

Until then, with every disappointment, take heart. Just try to keep in mind that your best opportunity is making its way to you. Slowly, maybe. But surely.

CHAPTER 18

Is That New Job You're Considering in an HR-Friendly Company?

I don't think anyone still buys that old line, "People are our best assets" (even though at its heart it's absolutely true). And most companies know better than to open with that bromide. If that's the best your potential employer can do and say to attract you, you might consider moving on. Quickly.

Take heart. This is truly the Golden Age of HR, and, as you search for your new job, you shouldn't have any trouble finding companies that completely understand how crucial people truly are to the company's long-term objectives. Still, there is a range of HR-friendliness among even the most evolved companies. Depending upon how much energy you are willing to devote to transforming a relatively HR-indifferent corporate culture, these hallmarks of an HR-friendly company will help you decide whether a particular company is for you.

Before You Even Go to the Company

Look at the company's web site first. Does it have a section that celebrates people and their contributions? Does the annual report focus just on the numbers and statistics, or are there pictures of the employees in the report? Does the CEO's letter mention the achievements and accomplishments of the company's people? If you don't see any clue that the organization's overall agenda includes recognizing and celebrating its talent, then it's probably not much of a people organization.

While you're online, check out the employee gripe groups. But don't take them completely seriously. They're good for gauging general trends and common issues, and for understanding what people are thinking and saying about the company. But it's also important to understand that any company is going to have dissenters and naysayers, especially when the company is undergoing a drastic change. And it can be especially destructive when the comments get personal. I've read some terrible things online about people I know who are trying their best to do the right thing. There are two sides to every story, and there will always be people committed to seeing how an issue hurts them rather than understanding how it's going to make the company get better.

Look for signs that the company is determined to attract and hire the best-in-class. Read local newspapers, business magazines, and the *Wall Street Journal* to get the background on the CEO, the senior leadership team, and the board of directors. These days you can find out just about everything you need to know about an executive online. You can find speeches, articles, résumés, salary, stock trades, and personal details. Find out where the company's leaders have come from. People bring with them what they've learned at their last employer. Those habits, principles, and assumptions will eventually leach into the system of their new organization. So you can find out a great deal about where the company is going by determining where its leaders have been. Find out what their growth and development expectations are for the company. If you see that they are making a concerted effort to hire the best, then you know that they have solid respect for the way HR can help them fulfill their ambitions.

Research the company's accounting practices. Just as this is the Golden Age for HR, it's also a stressful time for accountants, CFOs, and others who are entrusted with the financial management of the company. You want to be sure that the company's methods are unimpeachable. How is the board of directors structured? Are there more outsiders than insiders? Is the board diverse and balanced in terms of directors' backgrounds and expertise? Who serves on the audit and compensation committees?

If you're considering a start-up, you already know that you're taking on an extra risk. But you don't have to go into it entirely unaware. Find out where the founders have been. Who are their investors? Is there an advisory group or board overseeing their actions? Do they have a track record of success in this particular industry? Are they hands-on advisers as well? You will have a blank HR canvas on which to make your own mark. Don't go into this kind of opportunity for the "sure-thing payoff." But you will definitely be rewarded with the experience and opportunity of building HR and the business from scratch.

The most effective way of getting an understanding of the company in advance is to talk with people who already work there. Talk with your friends. See if they know someone who knows someone. That's where I found most of the information about the companies I've worked for. If you are well networked, you will probably know someone in HR at the company, maybe even the person you would be replacing. This person knows the best and the worst and will probably share the inside story. If you work in a big city where there is a popular after-hours night spot near the company, hang out there for a while. Strike up conversations with the people there. Also talk to the consultants, headhunters, vendors, lawyers, etc., who do business with the potential employer.

The Day of the Interview

Who will you be interviewing with? You should expect to be speaking with those who would be your key customers. If you're interviewing for the top job in HR, you should be interviewing with the top team:

the chairman, the CEO, the CFO, the COO, or operational leaders. You should be talking to all the key leaders in the company. If they don't think you're important enough to spend time with, that reflects their attitude toward the HR function.

If you're interviewing for the HR manager for a product line or business unit, you should be talking to the business leader of the line, the financial manager, and the engineer. If you're interviewing for a recruiter position for the finance division, you should be speaking with the CFO and the accounting and financial leadership people. Insist on speaking with your key constituency—the people you will be working with every day.

It's a bad sign if you're interviewing only with HR. If you don't speak with your key customers *and* with someone at a higher level than your position, you won't have a strong picture of what's expected of you.

As you enter the building, take a look at the reception area. What's in the lobby? What is the company showcasing? What is it proud of? How does the atmosphere of the lobby reflect the company's culture? As I've made the rounds of job interviews, I've sat in lobbies that felt so formal and uncomfortable that I immediately had serious doubts as to whether I could be myself in such a stark and rigid culture. In contrast, the lobby at Yahoo!'s headquarters greets its visitors with a huge purple cow, and the common areas are furnished with big jazzy purple and yellow chairs. Now that was a place where I knew I could laugh out loud in the hallways! There's a store off to the side where you can buy cool Yahoo! merchandise and a coffee bar toward the back where you can pick up a free coffee or latte or play a round of foosball. Besides the influence of the free-flowing caffeine, there's an upbeat, energized feel to the air, something that can come only from people who are enjoying their work and who know that they're equally appreciated by the company.

Don't draw quick conclusions from the appearance, though. I once went to an interview at a large retail company. The offices had not been updated for quite some time, and everything seemed drab and dull. But the people who greeted me were so friendly and made me feel so welcome that I knew right away that the physical appearance of the offices didn't reflect the company's culture. Not surprisingly, I discovered during the interview that the company was finishing up construction on a brand new campus and would soon be moving.

Where is the HR department physically located? An HR-friendly company makes sure that HR is easily accessible to where the action is in the workplace. HR has to be very easy for people to get to, or it disappears. Every company I've ever worked for put the HR department in the lobby. It was the very first office you saw once you entered the premises.

Several years ago I visited a company that was very proud of its innovative, state-of-the-art employee service center. While the people I was visiting were bragging about it, they made a special point of telling me that the doors to the service center were locked. No employees could get in there, the rationale being that, "Our employees should only *call* the service center. They shouldn't come in person." My hosts then went on to tell me, "Now that we no longer have to meet face to face with people, we take less time and are more efficient." I left that company with the question, "What does it say about the HR department when it's actually trying to keep people out of HR?"

When we created our service center at Southwest, we did have a call center, but we also had a big sign that was very welcoming. We made sure that there were places for people to sit and meet privately with People Department representatives. There are employees who will fly to our service centers to meet with a person face to face. If this is what they need to have in order to feel good about their transactions with HR, it is Southwest's job to make sure they get it.

During the Interview Itself

Are the people you interview with current on the pressing HR issues in the company? Can the senior leadership describe what has been accomplished so far in HR, what hasn't been, and why? Are all the people saying pretty much the same things? Or is there a big discrepancy in opinions?

I once interviewed with nine people in one day at a certain company, which shall remain nameless for an obvious reason. One of the people said to me, "Don't believe what the CEO tells you about the people agenda. It's a lot of talk and no action." That didn't necessarily turn me off to the company, but it did give me a clue that the challenge would be greater than the senior leadership had painted it as being.

Likewise, a hostile environment isn't necessarily a bad thing. In this particular case, I noted the inconsistency and considered several interpretations. One was that the previous HR head hadn't had the CEO's confidence, and so no progress could be made. Another possible meaning was that there weren't enough people or resources to make the changes. I kept my mind and my ears open.

If the company is telling you that it wants to change, find out what's driving the desire for change. The greatest change agent is pain. If the company suffers enough pain, it may want to change its ways. Does the senior leadership know the source of that pain? Is it high turnover rates? Is it a lawsuit? Is it low productivity?

If the leaders know the source of their pain, they may have a clear understanding of how HR can provide relief. That would make them HR-friendly.

Also listen carefully to the nature of the questions that people ask. If they're asking you all about administrative issues and not giving you the chance to discuss strategic aspects of HR, that should be a clue that your prospects at this particular company may be limited. Almost every company I've interviewed with says, "We want all these strategic things, but we need to get our turnover down or the recruitment time reduced." Almost every company has some basic elements of HR that it needs to address.

How do the people you interview with treat one another? Sure, companies may say, "People are our best assets," but how they treat one another tells you whether that philosophy is embedded in the culture. During one interview with a company president, the chairman barged into the meeting and interrupted our conversation without excusing himself, or even introducing himself to me. He was completely rude both to the president and to me. My thought was, "What a jerk." And I decided right then and there not to consider that opportunity any longer.

Ask for copies of company newsletters or other internal communications. This will tell you what the company is celebrating and how it recognizes individual contributions. Is it all about the senior team, or do you see evidence of people making significant contributions at all levels? Does it value long-time service, or do newcomers seem to be the most celebrated? Are diverse employees represented?

As careful as you are about interviewing job candidates, you must be equally discerning when you are investigating the possibility of changing jobs yourself. You know better than to buy the "people are our best assets" line without seeing evidence that backs that up.

CHAPTER 19

Welcome Aboard!
(And Watch Your Step!)

I suppose it will surprise no one to hear that I was in for a major culture shock when I decided to leave Southwest Airlines after thirteen years (and Dallas, where I had lived for twenty-nine years) and move to Silicon Valley to work for Yahoo!. True, some things were the same. Both companies are world-class industry leaders that are still heavily influenced by their founders on a daily basis and are animated by some of the most talented and dedicated employees you could hope to find anywhere. And both are energized by a clear vision of their future and how the company is going to change the world in its own way. But their cultures are completely different. The employees in Silicon Valley are unlike anything I'd ever seen before, in terms of their aggressiveness and expectations. Even the clock seems to run faster out here. If you don't get it done yesterday, "on time" is already too late. I had read about this strange place called Silicon Valley, and now I sometimes feel like I'm standing in highway traffic, with events, projects, and people whizzing all around me. But at least I wasn't surprised. And I came prepared to adjust to the culture change on a much deeper level than the obvious externals.

I knew enough from my previous years helping newly hired managers integrate themselves into their new jobs that the early days of a new job are crucial to your long-term success at the new company. No matter where you work, more than ever before, you get only one chance to make a good first impression. And I've seen many talented, well-intentioned new hires completely blow it on their first day. No one wants them to fail; after all, the company had invested huge amounts of money in finding and recruiting them. But, with the exception of a handful of really advanced organizations, no one is really equipped to help a newly hired leader take command. How do you conjure up a following among an already convened team (which probably had been functioning quite well on its own up until now, thank you very much) when you're still learning where the restroom is and whether you have to pay for your coffee? How do you walk into a conference room with a big grin on your face, saying, "Hey, y'all, follow me; I'm in charge now," when your new staff is still wondering what the heck really happened to your predecessor (and who might be next)?

If you've been in a senior HR role for very long, you've witnessed firsthand too many disappointments when people come on board. It's a tragic waste of time and money for everyone involved. As you look forward to beginning a new job—even if it's in the same industry or geographic location—the memories of those past failures can serve as cautionary tales to keep this same thing from happening to you.

There are steps you can take that will greatly improve your chances of a successful landing in your new position, performing up to your new company's expectations and smoothing the way to happier relationships with your new coworkers. You'll still be in for plenty of surprises, but with these steps, culture shock won't be one of them.

1. Start your cultural assimilation before you even start the interview process. Know what the key issues are and who the key players are before you go in for your first interview. Ask everyone you can think of for input: recruiters, friends who work at the company, consultants, and other vendors who serve the company. Ask them what their impressions and observations are. Compare and contrast their answers.

2. During the interview, make sure you understand what the senior team's expectations are from HR. If the team members disagree with one another, or with the CEO, you may be headed for trouble.

3. Also during the interview, ask the hiring committee to describe the culture, especially what is expected of you in the first three months, the first six months, and the first year. Some companies expect you to invest some time up front in developing relationships, establishing trust, and learning how things are done. If you behave in a more active, results-oriented way, you may be perceived as aggressive and pushy. Other companies want to start seeing results from you instantaneously. In this kind of culture, if you dillydally, taking the time to make friends and learn the way things are done, you may be perceived as lazy, unfocused, and unproductive.

It continues to surprise me that people coming into a company at senior levels don't always pick up on the nuances of corporate culture. Their egos are so big that they think they were hired to do the job a certain way (read: *theirs*), and that's the way they're going to do it. They don't stop to think: "How will this fit within the organization?"

4. Use the buddy system. Even if your position doesn't have an administrative assistant assigned to it on a permanent basis, the best thing you can do is ask if there is an assistant who has been there a long time (and therefore knows everyone and knows how to get things done) whom you can borrow for a few months to help you get settled. Such a person is your best source of information on whom you need to know inside the company, what the informal power structure is, and whether certain people like things to be done a certain way.

When I arrived at Yahoo!, there wasn't an assistant available. So I partnered with the HR manager who supported the HR department itself, Shelley Shaw. She was my buddy from Day One, setting up my schedule for me, setting up appointments for me well before I had even started. And explaining cultural nuances as I went along.

5. Let your family know that they're on their own for a while. Expect to have less of a private life for six months to a full year. If this isn't something your family can work around, think long and hard about whether you want to take on the challenge of a new, demanding job.

6. If your new company has multiple locations, get out and meet everyone right away. Schedule your travel before the people at your office get used to having you around and your workload piles up. Your work with locations around the country (or the world) will go much more smoothly if you've spent time with all your HR counterparts and other colleagues.

7. If the company culture will allow it, make the tough decisions very early on and get them behind you. However, if you want to bring in a whole new team, do it in small doses. Otherwise you'll create an atmosphere of fear and resentment. Decide what you need to do the most (and the quickest). Pick one replacement who will make the most positive difference to you, and then wait another six months before adding the next replacement. The delay will be a small price to pay for building trust within your organization.

8. Seek out some quick wins. Meet with your constituents and ask them, "If I could fix one thing, so that after my first six months here you would think I'm just the greatest, what would that thing be?" When I started at Yahoo!, I asked that question, and one of the women in my department joked, "Can you fix the disgusting smell in the ladies room?" Apparently this had been an issue for more than a month, and it was, well, gross. So I called the head of facilities and described the problem, and got back a scientific discussion about what caused it and what could be done to fix it. It was a small thing, but it made a large statement to my team: I'm here to serve.

Whether you hit the ground running or invest the time you need to make deep and meaningful relationships with your new coworkers, what will successfully integrate you into your new position will be the same statement: "I'm here to serve."

New Leader Assimilation: Help Your New Hires Beat the Odds

Unfortunately, not every new leader you hire will have the advantage of having read this chapter. But, now that you have this understanding of the steps that all newly hired leaders can take to improve their chances of success, you can make a difference in their successful landing in your company.

A few years ago I heard about the full-day new leader assimilation process at General Electric from someone who had worked there and had helped to develop it. When I joined Yahoo!, I was glad to see that a number of our HR managers were already using the process successfully. These are the essential elements:

▪ When a new leader is hired, convene a meeting with that person's new team members during the first week. With the leader in the room, give all the team members the chance to introduce themselves and say a little bit about who they are and what they do.

▪ Then, with the leader *out* of the room, have the team answer these questions: What do we want the new leader to know about us? What do we expect of this new person? What are the burning issues in our department? What are our concerns about the new leader? What does the new leader need to know about us as a team? What do we do well? Where do we need improvement? What do we want to know about the new leader? What are the major obstacles the new leader will face? Put the answers on a flip chart—but make sure they're anonymous so that the leader won't later be able to connect the comments to any one specific team member.

▪ After a lunch break, reconvene the team with the leader, and go over the items on the flip chart. Give the new hire a chance to ask questions about the comments and explore the ways in which he or she can take quick action on some of the issues.

■ The new leader can now formulate an agenda for the first few months. This exercise can bring to the surface more issues in one day than weeks of one-on-one meetings. Dirty laundry is aired. And in this open, even light-hearted way, the team begins to gel. This discussion is a great way for the entire team to discover with the leader what some of the unspoken issues, misunderstandings, and disconnects are.

HR Is Your Company's Best Asset

Building a From-the-Heart
HR Function—And a World-Class
Organization, While You're at it

CHAPTER 20

It's About People, Not Widgets!

I was once a panelist during a symposium on the future of HR in Silicon Valley. One of my co-panelists, the head of HR for a heavily branded computer company, spoke passionately about the need for HR leaders to consider themselves vital manufacturers and suppliers of necessary inventory for their companies—that inventory, of course, being people. I understand what he was trying to convey in his message: that we should rise above the historical preconceptions of our profession and consider HR strategy an indispensable part of the overall business plan. We shouldn't, he said, be bogged down by the emotionalism that goes along with being *people* people.

Of course, he's right. But he kept using a term that I object to on the deepest level: *factory*. "We're a factory," he said. And what we manufacture is the inventory that is necessary to get the job done. Talk to me about factories and I picture widgets—identically stamped out pieces, without feelings or concerns of their own, created by an equally feelingless process to meet a business need. End of story.

I don't know about you, but I don't know a soul who welcomes being considered inventory, widgets, capability, or even a human resource, for that matter. I'm not even wild about the expression *human capital*, although I like it better than *human resources*. My problem with *capital* is that it reduces the company's humanity to a financial component, albeit an investment, that is easily described on a ledger sheet.

Personally, I prefer the word *talent*, especially in today's business environment, when companies depend more than ever on the unique contributions, passion, commitment, and heart of every single individual within them. Each company's overall presence in the world is unique precisely because of the unique abilities of its people. This brings to mind the Hollywood model of building up the people side of doing business. If we were casting a movie or a play, we would look for people with a distinct set of styles, expressions, and circumstances, and even the ability to cast a spell over the audience—only in business it would be a different kind of magic, creating something inspired and wonderful that didn't exist before.

Before he started every scene, actor Jack Lemmon would whisper to himself, "Magic time!" That bit of whimsy didn't take away from his professionalism, it tapped into his talent. Isn't that more inspiring than, "Okay, crank up the factory!"

Just bear in mind that the machine is there to help you cultivate talent, not to stamp out widgets. Even Hollywood has processes for identifying an extraordinary talent and bringing it on board. Hollywood thrives because of its talent machine. So can you. Here's how.

Make Hiring Great People a Top Business Objective

Hiring great people should be one of the four or five things that your company consistently does well—and is famous for. Great people attract other great people because great people only want to work with great people. This principle should be one of your most publicized public relations messages. Make sure your annual report emphasizes that getting, keeping, and growing the right people are essential elements of your business's guiding principles. If this isn't at the top of the business agenda, department leaders will hire new employees according to their own varying standards. And you will lose the power of the common standard.

Have a Single Process for Delivering the Right Kinds of People That's Consistent Throughout All Your Locations

Use the same system for selecting the best candidates, put them through the same interview procedures, and deliver the same basic kinds of training. At Southwest we would recruit 4,000 to 6,000 employees a year in our locations all over the country. Whether the candidates were in Portland, Oregon; Manchester, New Hampshire; Fort Lauderdale, Florida; or Phoenix, Arizona, their experience with us would be the same.

Hire the Person, Not the Résumé

What most companies do is bring in a batch of candidates who have been identified as generally qualified by some form of résumé assessment process. Then the conversation continues to be résumé-focused, concentrating on skills and accomplishments. Instead, the conversation should bring out the whole person, especially the way that person works with others. The questions should be along the lines of "How did you work with your team?" "Who was the person you mentored who had the best success?"

Discriminate

No, I don't mean that you should discriminate against candidates on the basis of race, sex, age, disability, or veteran status. But because of the excellent laws that are in place to prevent you from discriminating in these ways, you and your HR staff may have been trained to focus solely on how well résumés match the job specifications.

There's no law, however, that says that you can't discriminate on the basis of someone's attitude or someone's ability to fit into the team. Your Number One nonnegotiable should be your cultural fit. If you hire people who don't fit, no matter how good those people are, or even if one of them is the best technical guru on earth, if they're not going to fit into your culture, they're not going to be successful. Fit is everything.

It's certainly not about money. At Southwest we deliberately saw to it that money wasn't the key attraction of working at the airline. If you offered a job that paid the most money in the world, you would have candidates who were looking only for money. We wanted people who were looking for a stable career, who were enthusiastic about working for a company with a unique culture, who thought the airline business was exciting. As a result, Southwest has an extraordinary community of employees who love their jobs. I'd look at the ramp agents hoisting luggage into the belly of planes in 110-degree heat during a Las Vegas summer and ask myself: How do these people do such hard work and love it so much? They did. We made sure we hired athletic people who loved the energetic, fun culture of Southwest, combined with the chance to do great physical work outside.

Cut Down on Your Workload; Give Candidates the Chance to Self-Select

When you make your corporate culture famous through all your public messaging vehicles, people will know whether they want to work for your company before they even send you their résumé. The stronger you make that message, the fewer the number of bad fits you'll have to weed out from the résumé stacks. At Southwest we made sure our message was very strong. Our ads in magazines and on billboards made our culture unmistakable. One ad featured CEO Herb Kelleher in an Elvis suit. The caption read: "Work in a place where Elvis has been spotted." And at the bottom of the ad it read: "But if you see him dressed as Ethel Merman, just ignore him. We're trying to cure him of that." Anyone who reads that ad is going to have no doubt that this is a zany kind of company. If readers find it silly and dumb, I'd say the chances are very good that Southwest wouldn't be the best place for them to work.

When we first came out with our new uniforms of shorts and golf shirts, we published a photograph of a flight attendant, shot from her feet to her waist. The ad read: "Work at a place where wearing pants is optional." Again, the underlying message was, "If you want a more casual atmosphere, where you can have fun and be part of a team, think about joining Southwest Airlines." If you found that inappropriate for a workplace setting, then you probably wouldn't apply to Southwest to begin with.

At Yahoo! we're going through the process of identifying what makes a "Yahoo!" in the current environment. We're looking for nice, smart people who are confident and innovative. And they need to be willing to speak their minds. We want people who don't need to have their jobs or even their future defined, who can take charge and make things happen, even when they're in uncharted territory. That's a lot to fit into our culture, and our main job is capturing those qualities and expressing them to the world in exciting and attractive branding messages.

Link your company's mission to a cause that employees can embrace. There's nothing more motivating, focusing, and energizing than knowing that you're making a difference in the world. It has to be about more than just doing the job. It has to be about making the world a better place in some way. Mary Kay Cosmetics makes products that help women be beautiful, and it also helps women to be self-sufficient by working on their own out of their homes. Mary Kay has some of the highest-paid women in business today, and everyone working in corporate headquarters can draw satisfaction from knowing that they are helping to make a real difference in the lives of women and their families around the world.

At Recognition, a business-to-business enterprise that wasn't nearly as sexy, we made computer transport equipment that made companies more efficient by processing high volumes of data and paperwork. We were the first to provide optical character recognition technology, which is obsolete today but was the very latest *cool thing* in its heyday. Banks, post offices, and airlines all used the technology. And while it might be hard at first to connect a cause to such a dry piece of technology, reminding employees that Recognition technology helps businesses be successful went hand in hand with reminding them that successful businesses help people be successful.

At Southwest we linked our HR programming work with our Freedom brand. Southwest Airlines' external brand was "A Symbol of Freedom," and our internal brand was "At Southwest freedom begins with me." We knew that if Southwest didn't exist, the whole country would be paying exorbitant prices for airfares. And we could prove it. Before Southwest was in business, only one out of every four Americans flew. Once we entered the industry with our mission of providing affordable airfares, three out of every four Americans flew. Every time we entered a new market, something called *the Southwest effect* would take place: Other airlines would discount at least some of their seats to match our fares. How does this translate to Southwest employees? They know that people from coast to coast have the freedom to go to that wedding they might have missed otherwise, to see their childhood friends, to go to that jazz festival, to attend that graduation, even to be there for that funeral—all those events and opportunities that make life rich and rewarding are now within reach of everyday Americans who wouldn't have otherwise been able to be there.

No matter what your company is or what your employees do, you have a cause. And that cause can fuel their excitement and commitment regardless of the ups and downs of the marketplace or the economy. Their enthusiasm is the real fuel for your talent machine. It will keep your business in perpetual motion.

**Building a From-the-Heart
HR Function—And a World-Class
Organization, While You're at it**

CHAPTER 21

The Nuts and Bolts of the Talent Machine

If you're attracted to the HR-from-the-heart principle that is the foundation of this entire book, you might find this nuts-and-bolts idea troublesome. True, there's a lovely romance attached to the traditional right-time–right-place love matches between an employer and the perfect candidate. But if you look behind the curtain of even the most epic love matches in history, you'll find at least one player who is using his or her head.

Use your head. This isn't romance, anyway. This is serious business, with millions of dollars and hundreds or thousands of lives at stake. The talent management process requires extreme discipline and commitment on the part of both HR and the entire enterprise. At Southwest, I often described our hiring philosophy as a religion, meaning that it was so central to our being that there could be no compromise. It was one of our best practices, it was one of our overall corporate objectives, and it had the full support of leaders at all levels. Install these nuts and bolts into your talent machine, and you'll be able to recruit great talent that you'll love into great jobs that they'll love.

Employee Referrals

No matter what the organization may be, employee referrals are the most valuable source of talent. At Yahoo! half of our employees come to us through a personal introduction by someone who already works here. This makes all the sense in the world. Friends seek each other out for that nebulous quality that we are all looking for: fit. As in that famous Amway recruiting chart, for every single circle that represents an employee, there are at least five additional circles of likely candidates attached to that circle. And for each of those five, there are five more, and so on and so on.

Turn every employee in your organization into a recruiter. If your employees love their work and the company, they're going to be recruiting for you anyway. But there are ways you can pump up the process now and then. For instance, you can pay for it. At Southwest we had an ongoing program called "BYOB" (Bring Your Own Buddy) where we'd offer a free ticket on Southwest for each new hire that came from an employee referral. For hard-to-hire positions, we would offer a cash award. But these programs would get stale, so we had to kick things up a notch by occasionally offering well-publicized contests in which we had a drawing from the names of employees who had successfully referred a candidate. The lucky winner of the drawing would receive a fabulous prize, such as a computer system or a big screen TV.

These programs don't have to cost a lot of money. At the height of the economic boom, we printed little business cards that looked like miniature versions of the plastic boarding coupons that Southwest is famous—or infamous—for. (Southwest discontinued using these cards after September 11 for security and efficiency reasons.) Each card carried the message that Southwest was looking for more employees, along with information on how to apply online or where to send a résumé. We mailed five cards to each employee, with a request to help us find great people. We asked them to hand out the

110

cards to people who gave them excellent customer service: the cashier at the supermarket, the ticket taker at the movies, the waiter, anyone the employees felt especially good about. The employees kept asking us for more and more of those cards. And soon it became a way of life. No one made a penny from this program, or won a fabulous prize. They did it because it felt good to be so active in building the company with terrific customer service people.

Public Relations

The Southwest PR team taught me well how incredibly valuable the word on the street is for finding and recruiting great people. If you can have well-placed articles and television or radio coverage about who you are as an employer and where you're hiring, more people will respond to those stories than will respond to ads that you pay for.

Before the Y2K systems overhaul, we had a huge need for IT professionals. So we decided we'd try to recruit from our customers by running an ad in our frequent flyer newsletter. The deal was, send us a résumé of someone you know with certain IT skills and you'll be entered in a contest for a free computer. We received about 2,000 résumés as a result (and one complaint from an IT executive who said that we were trying to steal her employees and therefore she would never fly Southwest again—so you have to be careful about these things). The number of résumés was mildly disappointing, but the ripple effect was beyond our wildest dreams.

It didn't occur to us that some of our frequent flyers were reporters. One of those reporters was a business journalist who read the ad and thought it was a great story. The next thing we knew, there were articles about the ad in the *Arizona Republic,* the *Los Angeles Times*; and the *Dallas Morning News*—which happened to serve the location where we had IT openings. Then a local television network affiliate saw the newspaper articles and came out to film our computer room, interview me and the IT employees, and show what kind of technology we were working on. We got far more résumés in response to the news coverage of our campaign than we got from the campaign itself.

Use the Power of the Internet

Your web site is your most powerful way to let prospective employees know what you are looking for. Here you can post your message, indicate what types of people you are looking for, give your candidates a way to apply online, and begin an interactive relationship with candidates. Use your advertising dollars to promote your web site rather than specific job openings. Once you have an established employment brand, people will flock to you. Online recruiting has changed the way we search for job seekers. Rather than placing an ad in one publication that is stale the next day, we can now run online job ads that reach across the globe. New technology is created daily that uses artificial intelligence to help match job requirements with skills. Technology advances now make it possible to find the elusive passive job seeker and prequalify candidates.

Know Who You're Going to Want Long Before You Actually Want Them

Most companies launch their recruiting process from a standing start, which means that they're too late before they've even begun. Your ideal goal is to have the candidate ready the day the job opens. The longer a job is open, the higher the probability that you will make a hiring mistake. When hiring managers are desperate to fill a position, it is just human nature that hiring standards will be compromised. Using the dreaded factory metaphor, plant managers know at the beginning of every year or season what the necessary inventory of parts, supplies, and materials must be to get the job done over time. Likewise, *your* plant should have a talent plan. What is the level of talent that you'll be requiring at what points throughout the upcoming months? How many people will you be needing? What are the knowns? What are the unknowns?

This approach requires a formula that will evolve and be refined over time. However, there are fundamental variables that you can use right away. Start with the predictable patterns of growth that can be seen historically in your company. If you work at a chain of stores, for example, you know that growth happens when you open a new location. Look back at your records to see how many people you typically hire to accommodate that kind of expansion. Don't limit your formula to the extra number of sales associates; remember to factor in the additional people hours at headquarters. At Southwest our growth was most often represented by the purchase of a new plane. When we ordered a new plane, we knew we'd need a certain number of pilots, flight attendants, and ground crew. Our main problem was that we couldn't always be sure *where* we'd need them—especially the ground crew. Seattle? Las Vegas? Providence? Baltimore? That part might take some last-minute finessing, but we had made our lives that much easier because we had planned ahead as much as we could.

Hire Mainly at the Entry Level and Promote From Within

This philosophy has several advantages: It perpetuates your culture, it encourages your people to be constantly learning and growing, it cultivates loyalty, and it keeps the knowledge inside. It is also a great way to build the company from the ground up in that for each job above the entry-level positions, there should be sharp, custom-trained, and custom-developed entry-level people who are ready to move up into it. If you do this, you should never suffer a severe talent shortage. And you may not even have to engage in the talent war that is raging outside your walls. (At least not as much—no matter how excellent the workplace culture may be, turnover will always be with us to some extent. The ideal is to keep that extent minimal and as healthy as possible.)

Make the most of this process by installing an internal hiring process that is just as rigorous as your external system. Post all jobs above the entry level internally so that your employees have the first chance to fill them. Create career development initiatives that prepare people to take charge of their own careers and give them the tools and skills that they need in order to qualify for the next likely opportunities. Be sure to create a culture in which going after new opportunities doesn't put employees' current jobs at risk. In many companies, if a boss gets wind of the fact that an employee is taking action to move on and up, that boss may make life very difficult for that employee. A supervisor may give an employee a lousy recommendation, either as retribution for perceived disloyalty or to keep the employee from advancing out of that department. Even in the best of companies, a certain amount of possessiveness can occur. So try to help supervisors understand that the greatest compliment to them is that they have groomed someone to be ready for advancement. Reward them accordingly.

Likewise, make sure it's safe for employees to try for a promotion and then not get it. In typical situations, employees may be reluctant to consider internal job changes, because they know that if they fail to receive the offer, they will have to keep working for a boss who knows that they attempted to leave. Under the best of circumstances, the potential feeling of failure and embarrassment can discourage talented employees from taking the risk. Under the worst of circumstances, a vengeful boss can make their lives miserable as they try to settle back into their current job. For every new job opportunity, you're going to have many disappointed hopefuls returning to their original job and only one successful candidate who gets to make the move. Make absolutely certain that all bosses welcome their employees back.

Also make sure that bosses don't cut loose troublesome employees just because they don't want to be bothered with them anymore. The internal hiring process can be misused as a recycling program for poor performers and misfits. If you don't want that kind of waste, you must have a discipline in place that says, "We don't pass a problem employee on to another manager." If an employee has issues, the manager should work those out before approving the move. Make your managers commit to that principle, perhaps by signing a contract that says, "I am recommending this person for this job. And if the person is not selected, I will be happy to take her or him back."

Aggressively Seek Out the Stars

There is a whole new class of employee out there who defies any kind of prefabricated job description and whose résumé your recruitment software would spit out, as it doesn't match any of the keywords you've programmed into the software. Yet, to quote Rodgers and Hammerstein, "once you have found them, never let them go." These individuals have always been with us, but they achieved critical mass during the last boom economy, when they were generally assembled under the category Free Agent Nation. They may have dropped out of the conventional employment track—especially those who were among the first to recognize that the employment contract was dead and that there was a big market for project-based work for a variety of companies and clients. Or they may have stayed inside the employment world but have dedicated themselves to a purpose, a profession, or an industry. Those are the ones who have been writing books, who have been speaking at conferences, who have been consulting independently. They may also be the ones who, for the right opportunity, would welcome the chance to work at your company. Make sure there's room in your talent plan to slow down, attract, and grab these thought leaders when they come into your line of vision.

Where do you find these visionary mavericks? They may be regulars at your trade association meetings. Or they may be speakers, or authors, or often quoted in articles. Find a way to bring them in for a get-acquainted conversation. It's very possible—maybe even likely—that they will welcome the opportunity to contribute their talent to the cause that your company stands for. If, after careful consideration, you decide you want one of these people, but there's no officially open position available for the person to step into, create one. That newly created title could be the hot spot for innovation and leadership that will put your company on the map. (In addition, if you're known for hiring stars, more stars will gravitate to your company.)

But move carefully with this group. Just because someone is a star doesn't mean that that person will shine brightly inside your particular corporate culture. Even though the person is great and you're great, you may not end up being all that great together—especially if your culture isn't so wild about the maverick approach to life and work.

Don't Forget the Stars You Already Have in Your Ranks

Throughout your organization, you have people who are essential to the future of your business. These people would be difficult if not impossible to replace. They are developing new products, they are keeping your most important customers happy, they have deep institutional knowledge, and they are rising to positions of leadership. Place a special emphasis on nurturing these stars. It should be deliberate and should include high-touch executive attention, career development opportunities, more frequent compensation reviews, more stock options, or whatever else is important to keep these folks engaged.

Remember the Important Link Between Hiring Talent and Growing Talent

Staffing and organizational development should be attached at the hip. Their roles, when they are combined as a function, are talent acquisition and talent development. The process of talent management is much more than just matching people with job requisitions. The greatest organizations invest in career development, leadership development, and internal career pathing. Not only is their external online job site rich with branded information for external job seekers, but their *internal* placement site is richer and better and includes online learning and developmental opportunities. Recruiters don't just interview external candidates who are seeking to join the company, they also interview qualified internal candidates who have been working toward the next step in their career. And they help people move through traditional and nontraditional roles and responsibilities. Recruiters are responsible for selecting new leaders in partnership with department heads. They are available as career coaches, while learning facilitators design and deliver opportunities for internal candidates to prepare for their next steps and to meet the organization's needs. Recruiters working with learning facilitators help leaders to mentor their team members and develop the competencies that will be needed in the future.

To create a talent machine where there previously was none will require a significant culture shift that will take some time, some patience, and some tolerance for missteps here and there. It's worth the investment. What you will get in return is a smoothly functioning process of talent acquisition and development with just-in-time delivery.

Building a From-the-Heart
HR Function—And a World-Class
Organization, While You're at it

CHAPTER 22

HR Does *Not* Create Culture

It's a common mistake to look to HR as the source from which all corporate culture flows. I suppose it's understandable. Culture is, after all, people. And people are HR's domain, right? Many CEOs don't want to be bothered with such a pesky, hard-to-measure element as *culture*, so they delegate it to HR, saying, "You take care of it." It isn't at the top of the business agenda, and everyone thinks it's HR's problem. But it's actually everyone's problem and responsibility.

Culture does have its roots in people, it's true. But those people are the founders of the organization. Whether they realized it or not, the company's culture began in those very first hours when a dream of something new and wonderful started taking shape on a cocktail napkin or in a computer file. It's a rare entrepreneur who is thinking about HR at that stage! And few entrepreneurs begin their dream companies by describing from the start what the culture of those companies will be. But still, in those early days, they were creating just that—their new company's culture. When Southwest's most notorious CEO, Herb Kelleher, was putting his first flight attendants in hot pants, was he thinking about culture? I doubt it. When Bill

Hewlett and David Packard were tinkering in their garage, was culture on their minds? Nope, the next great idea was. But they were creating culture anyway. When Jerry Yang and David Filo were procrastinating on their Ph.D. dissertations and developing a Web directory from their Stanford University trailer, were they thinking about the culture of the as-yet-unestablished Yahoo!—a company that would very quickly employ thousands of people around the world? No. I suspect they were actually thinking, "We really ought to stop this and get back to our studies." Corporate culture is never "top of mind" when creative genius is busy making something that didn't exist an hour ago.

The founders of companies begin with their own personal set of values, beliefs, and behaviors that shape their initial work environment. More likely than not, the first group of employees shares those values, and a culture begins to evolve, rather than being deliberately created. Certain values, behaviors, work ethics, and communication channels become central to the way things get done. The business survives and grows because the group of original employees develops an indomitable drive to succeed. Visionary leaders emerge to lead in true entrepreneurial style, reflecting the core cultural attributes. Since few start-ups have the foresight to invest in HR, these leaders handle the people issues—or these responsibilities are ignored altogether. But still, many start-ups are celebrated for their exciting culture. Somehow this culture happens without the presence of HR.

HR usually arrives on the scene as the enterprise achieves a successful formula for delivering results and grows to such an extent that it enters a new phase. Now there is a need to compete for talent, focus on the working environment, grow and develop new skills, formalize reward systems, and comply with applicable regulations. These key activities allow HR to lead and drive the development of a company's culture, but not to *create* that culture. At this stage, the best companies recognize the importance of a strong positive culture as a sustainable competitive advantage, and every employee becomes a "keeper of the culture."

Much has been written on how organizations transform or change their cultures. As those who have embarked on cultural reengineering efforts know, an established culture is persistent. Once a culture exists, it is difficult to change. Changing it involves changing behaviors and unspoken assumptions within the entire workforce. To effect true cultural transformation, the structure and every system and process must reinforce the aspirational culture. All leaders must embrace new attitudes and conduct their activities in new and different ways—even if they feel that they are threatened personally with loss of power or loss of their jobs. HR leaders cannot go it alone in these endeavors. Changing the culture requires the efforts of everyone in the enterprise. Rather than arriving at this point, it is better work to shape the culture through a natural evolution from the very beginning.

The best and most admired mature organizations keep culture at the top of the business agenda. These organizations recognize the importance of an evolving culture. In fact, a hallmark of companies that survive and thrive is a culture that is flexible and adaptable.

As the HR leader, your role is to ascertain what the culture *is* and how it adds to or detracts from the company's objectives. Does the culture attract, retain, and engage top talent? What are the good parts of your company's culture? An upbeat environment that's based on team spirit? A strong emphasis on open communication? An innovative culture that's built on risk and creativity? Or a culture that finds comfort and efficiency by relying on tradition and uniformity?

Conversely, what are some of the established cultural traits that no longer work for the company? Has your company matured into an established business with a heritage of known products but still encourages behaviors that were appropriate for its innovation stage? Have your customers matured and moved away from a maverick sense of counterculture, while your employees stay rooted in youthful exuberance? Or has the company fallen behind the times? Have the leaders deluded themselves into thinking that the organization continues to make its original values a way of life, while the employees feel disconnected from those values? How can you update the company's internal culture to stay current with your market, without losing your valued employees? Remember that it is much easier to change certain elements of a culture than to do a complete overhaul. Quick wins and small successes make additional efforts possible.

Finally, what aspects of your culture are actually cultural imperatives? What are the nonnegotiables inside your company that would immediately spit out people who somehow don't fit? At Southwest, for example, our culture was famously innovative and fun. That spirit wouldn't last a day in a banking culture. And likewise, if people I knew during my years serving the financial services facilities management industry tried to impose their strong top-down power structure on a Southwest team, they'd discover very quickly that they'd better loosen up . . . or pack up.

It's everyone's job to perpetuate the company culture. HR's unique way is through the recruitment, learning and development, and compensation programs that can drive, reinforce, and reward certain behaviors.

How HR Can Drive Culture

If your CEO says, "Fix our culture," don't take on the assignment all by yourself. Think about what you should do, what you can do, and, just as important, what you should pass on to other departments.

What HR Should Do

■ *Understand your current culture.* As we discussed, you need to know what behaviors work inside the company, which ones don't work, and what will best position the company to meet its future objectives. One way to achieve this is to conduct a cultural assessment or audit of your organization through employee surveys, focus groups, or interviews. Next, review your organization's history, leadership styles, and HR programs and look at practices in the industry to determine what currently drives and reinforces the culture. Finally, what is your customer experience? What cultural elements are obvious to customers? Is your culture aligned with your business strategy? Where are the disconnects? What needs to change?

■ *Develop a business case for cultural change.* Why is the change needed? How will the desired changes in culture support the business strategy?

■ *Work with the senior leadership team to define the aspirational culture.* Core values, desired behaviors, and shared vision are essential if a culture change effort is to succeed. Every leader must embrace the need to change, or it won't happen. Senior leaders must make new behaviors their way of life in order to reinforce desired change.

■ *Develop an agenda or action plan for enhancing the culture or bringing about change.* Start with the highest priorities and work on the toughest issues. If your culture is to become a way of life and be self-sustaining, every process must reinforce the core values and the culture.

■ *Communicate what needs to change and why.* Solicit input from people. Once the needed changes and processes for change are defined, tell people what is expected of them. Also make sure that everyone understands both the rewards for changing and the negative consequences of not changing.

■ *Hire for fit.* Identify the characteristics of people who exhibit those behaviors that you've identified as desirable. The people who fit and thrive in your culture will perpetuate that culture in everything they do. If you have to choose between a candidate who has better skills or knowledge but doesn't fit and a candidate who is slightly less qualified but fits culturally, choose the slightly less qualified person and provide the necessary training or on-the-job experience. For those who don't or won't fit into the culture, point them in the direction of finding other opportunities.

■ *Invest in new hire orientation training.* Be sure that every new employee knows what it will take to fit in and understands the cultural imperatives. Talk about the ways of working that lead to success and the ones that are the showstoppers.

■ *Create leadership talking points.* Be sure that every meeting, every training course, every communication piece includes cultural messages and reinforces the company's values, mission, traditions, and practices.

■ *Build an internal brand that supports the external brand.* Make a promise to deliver a consistent employee experience. Be sure that your employees know about the differentiating climate and the programs and services that will enhance their work lives and careers.

■ *Install compensation programs that reward preferred behaviors.* Your compensation and incentive programs should support the culture that you are working to reinforce. If your culture supports promotion from within, make sure your managers are measured and rewarded according to the developmental support they provide to their direct reports.

■ *Cultivate leaders who promote your culture.* What kind of leadership strengths and skills will perpetuate your culture down through the ranks? Who exhibits those assets early? Find them. Develop them. Invest in leadership development programs that reinforce cultural messages. Keep the good people, and get rid of those who are unable to pass the culture on.

What HR Can Do

■ *Keep telling the stories.* Every corporate history has a few legends. The long nights during the start-up phase. The "flat dinners," or pizzas keeping the entrepreneurs fueled into the early morning hours. That first dollar that's framed and hung over the cash register. Encourage people to tell those stories. Create "heroes" as central figures in the legends. Celebrate success, and, yes, celebrate failures. Demonstrate that people can survive and learn from their mistakes. Celebrations and events can reinforce the culture message.

■ *Make it fun.* Create contests and activities that enhance the culture. Decorate the office in inspiring ways. Dress up on Halloween. Give out valentines.

■ *Use your HR tools.* I learned early on at Southwest that communicating the benefits plan could be also be a primary source of key cultural messages. Every training class should reinforce the basic behaviors and values that reinforce the culture. Performance review forms should measure cultural fit as well as job performance.

■ *Form a culture committee.* Engage the help and support of a group of passionate, committed cross-functional team members to identify cultural disconnects and recommend remedies.

■ *Transform the organizational structure to enable change.* Find new ways to accomplish work tasks. Use teams for one-time projects. Broaden roles and responsibilities.

What HR Should Let Other Departments Do

No one should be locked out of the culture campaign. Just as the culture itself should permeate the entire organization, the entire organization should have a hand in perpetuating it. Corporate communications, advertising, and marketing should capture the culture message and spread it both internally and externally. New product development should manifest the cultural values in the way it responds to the marketplace demand with quality and service. The legal department should demonstrate the company culture by advising your corporate leaders on behaviors that are not only legal but also the right thing to do.

You're not solely responsible. You can do a lot to drive the culture and make it better. But no one department can force corporate culture on the rest of the company. You must achieve buy-in from everyone, from the CEO all the way down.

Building a From-the-Heart
HR Function—And a World-Class
Organization, While You're at it

CHAPTER 23

Internal Branding:
The Enchanting Power of
the People Promise

Try this simple experiment one night when you're home and there's nothing good on television, but you're really too tired to do anything more strenuous than stare at the tube. Don't watch the programs; watch the commercials instead. Notice how the major products are presented, especially in those mysterious pharmaceutical commercials. You're not quite sure what the drugs being advertised actually do. But you have no doubt that once you take them, your life will be full of sunny skies, green pastures full of blooming things, loads of friends, and long, romantic walks on beaches far, far away from the nearest bathroom.

These commercials aren't selling the pills. They're selling the results of the pills. They're selling the pill's promise—how much more you will get out of life (and all the emotional value that you associate with that message) if you take their pills. Commercials don't sell you the product; they sell you the meaning, the lifestyle, the transformation, the potential, the joy, the fulfillment that the product promises. This is the message that engages you, that enchants you, and that compels you to give the product a chance.

And this is the method that you can use to engage and enchant your employees. It is the meaning and the promise that lie behind their daily efforts that give their jobs a deeper resonance and compel commitment. And, borrowing a page from the advertising experts, you offer them this meaning and promise through branding.

In recent years, when recruiters were ferociously competing with one another for the available (and even unavailable) top talent, internal or employment branding was a powerful way for companies to differentiate themselves and their employment promise from their competitors. But even in down cycles, branding continues to hold its value as an important HR tool. It unifies employees under a shared sense of mission and values; it constantly broadcasts the message of meaning, and that message continues to attract other like-minded candidates who identify with the values that your company both stands for and offers. The communication of an employer brand using a consistent voice, look, feel, and tone—throughout the entire employment relationship—is the most powerful tool I have discovered. Branding is, in a very real sense, the oil in your talent machine. It helps keep all the many parts moving smoothly.

Southwest discovered the immense power of this kind of internal branding almost accidentally. When Herb stepped in as CEO of Southwest, one of the first things he decided to do was hire a new ad agency to put a fresh spin on our external marketing message. True to form, he hired a young, zany Texas-based start-up, GSD&M, and as a team the agency and Southwest's leadership asked themselves, "What do we have that differentiates us from our competitors?"

What Southwest had was "that certain Southwest spirit." Let's face it, all airlines have airplanes and fly from one city to another. Southwest was unique because of the spirit of our people. Our people at ticket counters, our reservations agents, our gate agents, our flight attendants were energetic, compassionate, caring, and smiling. Customers knew that our employees loved their jobs. And we decided to use that differentiator externally as our competitive advantage.

Consequently, we knew that if our employees were our secret weapon, we'd better make hiring one of our core competencies. If we were advertising that Southwest had that certain Southwest spirit, we needed to make sure that we had the systems in place to hire people who already had that spirit. So the people function was a core competitive competency from the early days.

Then Colleen Barrett, currently president and COO, smartly observed that if we were advertising that message of spirit to the customers, we should send the message internally as well. From that time on, each time we advertised a new slogan or tag line to the public, we had to make sure that everyone inside Southwest understood what it meant—what our *promise* was. This was a basic and obvious principle, but few companies link their external messaging with their internal messaging. And so the employees don't deliver the promise, the brand isn't built, and the company doesn't become strong. Colleen was determined to see that that didn't happen at Southwest.

Over the years, our marketing strategy became so effective that Southwest became a major national airline instead of a small regional carrier. So we needed a unifying national message. And we chose "Symbol of Freedom." As noted in Chapter 20, Southwest was making flying affordable for Americans. Before Southwest, only one out of every four Americans flew because flying was so expensive. Businesspeople (mostly men) traveled, but even business travel by air wasn't that prevalent in the early days of Southwest because it was too expensive for ordinary people. Because of Southwest's mission to deliver to Americans this freedom to fly, people could just get on airplanes and go at a very low cost.

Now we needed to have our employees catch the passion and power behind this vision of opening up travel to everyday Americans. So our marketing department came up with fantastic collateral materials, including an inspiring video and a Southwest Declaration of Independence, which we sent to everyone's home. We talked about freedom in everything we did. Our culture committee sponsored a creative "freedom tour" and sent an old-fashioned steamer trunk from city to city, with each city adding its own "symbol of freedom." Our internal communications department included the freedom message in every employee publication. Still, despite all our efforts, what the freedom spirit meant for individual employees didn't catch on as strongly as we had hoped. We knew we needed to better enroll our employees in this new vision.

With the help of Hewitt Associates, we embarked on one of the country's first internal branding projects, designed to marry the external message with an internal brand identity that really stuck. Our message was: "When you come to Southwest as an employee, you will have a feeling working here that you won't get anywhere else." Our challenge was to figure out a way of making this message *real*, not just another one-dimensional piece of propaganda.

Our first step was to convene a cross-function group of Southwest people from advertising, public relations, marketing, operations, and HR. We spent days in a room with flip charts, cataloging pages upon pages of answers to the simple question, "When you work at Southwest, what do you get that you wouldn't have if you worked somewhere else?" After compiling all the answers to that question, we grouped them into categories, which we presented to focus groups of employees for their reactions. When we finished, we had eight basic freedoms:

- To pursue good health

- To create financial security

- To learn and grow

- To make a positive difference

- To travel

- To work hard and have fun

- To create and innovate

- To stay connected

Like those emotionally engaging commercials we all see on television, we then translated these freedoms into outcomes, always linking those outcomes to the freedoms in all our messages. Working in partnership with everyone we could (our ad agencies, benefits consultants, employment partners, etc.), we created great employee-related products and services and tied them together under the Freedom theme.

For example, until we came up with this new internal branding approach, the whole retirement process was decentralized and confusing. A flight attendant I knew from the culture committee said that she had had to fly to headquarters four separate times to go through the various steps and paperwork necessary to retire. Furthermore, she told me, some people just want to privately explore the possibilities of retiring and to understand what it ultimately means, without actually having to publicly announce the fact that they're curious. A little privacy wouldn't be such a bad thing, she said. So we organized and simplified the entire retirement process. And we posted all the relevant information online so that employees could quietly do the research without letting the company know about it. We marketed our retirement program with an ad showing a Southwest seat with rocking chair runners under it. The slogan was, of course: You've earned the freedom to retire.

We also produced Freedom Expos, which were huge internal expositions, sort of like the exhibit hall at an HR conference. Every department was involved, with booths and demonstrations—all organized under the general theme of freedom. Attendees received a Comprehensive Freedom Planner, a canvas bag, and a T-shirt with the freedom icons. My favorite booth was the mechanics' booth, categorized under Freedom to Learn and Grow. These guys usually work at night, and they hardly ever get the chance to meet anyone else in the company. Here was their chance to show what they do, demonstrating different parts of an airplane and letting people pick up and examine $35,000 pieces of metal! It was like a gigantic county fair. But instead of blue-ribbon livestock, we were celebrating all the ingredients of the Southwest Spirit and the freedom that employees provided externally and received internally.

An advantage of branding is that it gives everyone the chance to take their own initiatives, as long as those initiatives respond to the overall theme. One day I was flying somewhere, and I was handed a cocktail napkin along with my drink. Normally these napkins are printed with a route map on one side and a marketing message on the other. This particular napkin had "Log on for Low Fares" on one side, and when I turned it over, I discovered a smiling face made from peanuts that said, "Freedom to be yourself is the freedom to be your best. Check out our great career opportunities at www.southwest.com." I was so surprised to see this! Probably some people in my department, in partnership with marketing or public relations, took it upon themselves to have these printed up. It made a strong connection between the internal and external brands. No one asked my permission to do this—which was just fine with me! They had the freedom to create and innovate!

Packaging the Brand Promise in Your Company

■ Understand what your external brand promise to your customers is and determine whether this is the message that your marketing, advertising, and public relations departments intend to continue using. If it is, fine. You can build your internal message on a foundation that has already been built to reach out to the public. If these departments are embarking on a messaging overhaul, use this opportunity to create a brand message that can be translated meaningfully both externally and internally.

■ Use the expertise and the techniques of your marketing, communications, advertising, and public relations people to comprehend how employees currently perceive the company, what they want, and how you can help them experience the company in a more positive way. Focus groups are one example of a classic marketing tool that will give you extraordinary insight.

■ Engage your employees in every stage of the process. To make sure that your messages sustain their meaning and credibility over time, keep your employees involved. Answer these three questions for employees:

What does the company stand for?

How will the company deliver on its stand, consistently?

How can I, as an employee, help my company succeed right now?

■ Choose powerful key phrases and link all your messages to them. Southwest has gotten a lot of mileage out of "freedom."

■ Keep it real. Develop a narrative proclamation of how your organization will carry out the promise and uphold the values in the employment relationship. Don't overpromise and underdeliver. Your brand promise should be powerful and emotionally evocative. But it also must be tightly connected (and connectable) to your employees' daily experience with the company.

■ The promise statement can be used on a day-to-day basis to inform and guide decisions that affect the employment relationship. All communication materials—from recruiting advertisements, to compensation and benefits, to retirement—follow the brand communication guidelines.

■ Just as you market the external brand externally, market the internal brand externally as well. Let the outside community, customers, and potential candidates know what it's like to work at your company. They'll be happier to buy from you when they know that your employees love their work. And you'll attract an enthusiastic mass of candidates who understand what you're trying to achieve and want to help you achieve it.

Building a From-the-Heart
HR Function—And a World-Class
Organization, While You're at it

CHAPTER 24

The Power of *People* to Make Your HR Branding Work

In 1989, with a new HR leader at Southwest, it was time to re-brand the HR function within Southwest Airlines. *Human resources* didn't work for us because that term implied that our employees were something that could be easily used up and then thrown away or replaced—a message that didn't fit with our mission and commitment to employees. One member of the group suggested *employee department*. But calling our people *employees* did not accurately reflect the value we placed upon them. One even suggested *folks*. Finally, the group settled on *people department*. I reluctantly had my business cards reprinted, and I cringed as I caught my colleagues rolling their eyes when they thought I couldn't see them. It took me a while to really appreciate the meaning behind the word *people* in our department heading, as opposed to *human resources*. At first I thought it was hokey. (I even worried about what my SHRM friends would say. At that point, they were just making the shift from *personnel* to *human resources*.) But I understood intellectually the spirit behind the change.

It wasn't until almost ten years later that I finally, most fully, understood the value and power of the word *people*. It was the day I said good-bye to Cindy Serniak for the last time. A long-time flight attendant, she had left Southwest after she married a pilot. But she was never far from our thoughts, and we weren't far from hers either. Later, after her divorce, she was involved in a terrible car accident and, as a quadriplegic, was confined to a motorized wheelchair. But that chair didn't confine Cindy. She returned to school, got a degree in counseling, and returned to work at Southwest, where we were all overjoyed to see her again. Starting out as a receptionist, she quickly moved up through the ranks and moved into the People Department.

One holiday we had special People Department denim shirts (along with a People Department logo designed just for us) made up as a gift to all the department employees. Everyone was thrilled because by then, the "people" moniker had taken hold. And because Cindy's condition made it inconvenient for her to wear shirts and slacks, she had her shirt tailored, adding a skirt and making it into a dress. And that's what she wore as she worked hard and moved up through the ranks to become a recruiter specializing in recruiting pilots and flight attendants.

Sadly, she suddenly died from complications of her condition. We were all shaken, and as with all funerals of Southwest people and their families, a delegation of Southwest employees attended. I, of course, was among them. I approached her open casket to say farewell and was thunderstruck to see what she was wearing. Of all the beautiful clothes in her closet, her family had chosen the garment that meant the most to her in her adult life: her People Department denim shirt. From that moment on, the word *people* carried a whole new weight of meaning and value to me. No matter what we call our departments, we are running organizations of people—not resources, not capital, not widgets. And we are a small part of every single person's large adventure of living, making a difference, finding a place in the world, and being able to look back when it is all over and think, "I spent my time well."

The word *people* still carries extra meaning for me when I compare it with other HR department–related titles. But it still confuses others. For a while I would get a call at least once a week from someone who wanted to know, "What is the difference between a people department and an HR department'? An HR director called one day and said, "My boss heard Herb speak at a luncheon in Seattle. He came back to the office and told me to change the name of my department. What do I do differently now?"

What is the practical difference between *human resources* and *people*? When we change the name of our department to *people*, does it really change the culture, the expectations, the customer service philosophy of the company toward its employees? I wasn't entirely sure, although I could certainly see how the change reflected (and then promoted) Southwest's own people philosophy. So, I decided to conduct a little survey of my HR colleagues in large corporations around the United States. While my academic friends would frown upon the statistical validity of my survey (or lack thereof), I wanted to find out which organizations were adopting a *people department* label, and what that change represented for their business philosophy. I asked the staff at the SHRM information center to produce for me a list of all members that had the word *people* in the title. After eliminating companies such as PeopleSoft and duplicates, I found 100 *people* people. I sent each a survey, and I got 20 responses.

Companies Represented

AT&T Wireless

Boeing

Cellular One

Compaq

Colgate Palmolive

The Dial Corporation

Herman Miller

KFC, USA., Inc.

Land O'Lakes, Inc.

Mapco

Nextlink

Racal Datacom, Inc.

Reno Air

Saturn Corporation

Sears, Roebuck & Co.

ServiceMaster

S.C. Johnson

Truegreen-Chemlawn

United Airlines

University of Alabama

Wal-Mart

Their main reasons for making the change were:

- A renewed interest in the needs, wishes, and overall satisfaction of their employees

- A shift in the whole paradigm or philosophy of the organization toward a more people-sensitive environment

- Mergers that created a "new culture"

What did they say that *people* signifies for the company?

- It serves as a constant reminder that the HR department is working to *serve* the people.

- It broadens the scope of the department, encompassing all functions having to do with people.

- It humanizes the profession.

- It defines employees as consultants, not task-doers.

- It brings a fresh approach, which attracts attention.

What are these companies doing differently as a result of the introduction of the *people* concept?

- Employees are now more involved in the decision-making process.

- The companies are more dedicated to their customers, both internal and external.

- They have experienced a deeper commitment to the philosophy of the *people* department.

- They have developed and implemented new hiring practices.

- They have more ongoing training and development programs.

- There is an increase in teamwork and job sharing.

- There are more proactive and improved business processes.

Every now and then our profession cycles through new labels to update (or upgrade) our identity and to remind us of our ultimate mission. When we made the shift from *personnel administration* to *human resources,* we were largely motivated by a desire to connect our activities more closely to the larger strategic corporate role and to disconnect ourselves from the lower-level administrative limitations we'd been associated with over the years.

Personally, I hope *people* catches on. It's not about *us* in the profession. It's about our customers. That is, after all, why we're here. Right?

Building a From-the-Heart HR Function—And a World-Class Organization, While You're at it

CHAPTER 25

Who Is Really HR's Customer?

HR is one of the most customer service–driven of all the departments in a company. There's just one small problem: As a profession, we can't agree on who the customer is.

"Who is really HR's customer?" That question has taken on an almost mystical quality, like that associated with brain teasers and Zen philosophies. "What is the sound of one hand clapping?" "Which came first: the chicken or the egg?" "Who is really HR's customer?"

For decades now that last question has been trotted out as an ice-breaker, as an annual dinner keynote theme, as a topic for break-out session discussion, and as the subject of many magazine articles.

Generally the answers break down in this way:

- The CEO (usually corporate leaders are fond of this answer)

- The shareholders

- The customers

- The employees

Heaven help you if you give the last of these answers in a group of senior HR executives. You'll be immediately pegged as idealistic, inexperienced, naive, or not leadership material. But in many ways, you are the one who's right. Most HR professionals I know never forget our important role as advocate for the employees, and we work ceaselessly to bring together the interests of the employees, the enterprise, and the stakeholders. However, in very senior groups, few will admit this perspective. And there you'll be, alone in a crowd, picking up on a chilly vibe and asking yourself, "What did I say? What did I say?"

There's a very good reason why this question has created so much discussion and argument over the years. It's based on a faulty, destructive, and unspoken assumption. And that is this:

"When the times are good, it's all very nice to be celebrated as an employee-friendly company. But one day we're destined to have to make a hard choice. And when that time comes, who's going to be the 'them,' and who's going to be the 'us'?"

When I'm asked to join in this talk, my answer is always, "The customers of the entire enterprise." When you regard everyone as a customer of the company (and therefore of your department), the answer becomes more a service-related philosophy that embraces everyone equally than a policy that puts the emphasis on one group over another. By *everyone* I mean the CEO, the shareholders, the board members, the point-of-purchase customers, the employees, and even vendors, consultants, and other outside groups that we partner with. And when you take this philosophy, you can't help but align HR's goals and deliverables with the company's goals and deliverables. And you'll naturally be operating in sync with the company as a whole.

At Southwest we operated on the main principle that our employees were Customer Number One. The external customers (the passengers) were Customer Number Two. This made exquisite sense; we were modeling the behaviors and allowing our employees to experience for themselves what our product was. Since our main product was customer service, we wanted to make sure that our employees were *very* familiar with our product.

Our success was completely dependent on our employees. And so we designed the entire company around treating the employees well and doing the right thing for them. Employees who know how it feels to receive excellent service know what it means to give it. And that's how Southwest Airlines developed its excellent customer service record.

Employees Are Investors, Too

For companies with employee stock ownership programs, this principle would appear to be self-evident. But I'm talking about something deeper here. With or without stock, employees are investing their lives with the company. There must always be a sense of psychic ownership among employees; they must know that what they're doing is more than just doing the job, that they're growing both their own personal future and the company's. With or without stock, when employees feel this level of connection to the company's long-term results, their own values and interests are going to be aligned with those of the shareholders (at least, with those of the shareholders who are in it for the long haul). They will be seeking the same kinds of return on investment. This is the mentality that you want to achieve throughout the company culture.

Not only are your employees invested psychically, but they can also drive the intangible aspects of your company's market valuation. This principle plays out in the form of real market value for the company. Over the last decade, investment analysts have been noticing that earnings aren't the only factor in determining shareholder value. Many companies with large market caps have them because of intangible elements, such as brand, reputation, employee relations, confidence, and trust. These intangibles come from excellent integrity, reputation, and customer service.

And these intangibles lead to great return on investment. According to the Great Place to Work Institute and its web site (www.greatplacetowork.com), $1,000 invested in companies that appear on its 100 Best Companies to Work For list returned an average of $8,188 over the ten-year span between 1992 and 2002, as compared with a $3,976 average return from companies on the Russell 2000 Index. According to the institute, "Using various profitability indicators, . . .

publicly traded 100 Best Companies consistently outperform major stock indices over the ten year periods preceding the publication of the 100 Best lists!" (http://greatplacetowork.com/gptw/business_benefits.html)

Your Vendors/Business Partners Are Customers, Too

When you have a strong customer service–driven culture, the smallest thing that doesn't quite match or fit can be a handicap in terms of the company's potential to achieve success. This principle goes for your outside vendors as well as your internal customers (the employees). The more companies use external business partners, vendors, suppliers, and consultants—and the stronger the companies' own internal cultures are—the more important it is going to be that your external partners operate with the same spirit of strong customer service. This idea may be easy to understand and believe when you're relaxed and reading this book. It's an entirely different matter when you're in the middle of your workday, you've got demands on all sides of you, and your day is interrupted by an eager salesperson with some "great ideas" on how you can spend your money.

Treating outside vendors kindly and politely is an excellent way to reinforce among your own employees the idea that when it comes to from-the-heart customer service, you mean business. They're watching what you say to and about sales callers, and they will take to heart the standards you establish. And, let's face it, even the most irritatingly aggressive salesperson may one day be a customer of your company. Or he or she might be a pal of the next hot recruit you try to woo.

When I was at Southwest, we actually had the suppliers themselves change the way they did business because of their experience working with us. We once became very frustrated by the poor customer service philosophy demonstrated by the service providers who were taking care of our employees. So we developed a "new hire" orientation program designed especially for our partners. Many of the same elements that all new hires are exposed to were featured in this program, especially the message that we consider our employees to be the Number One customer. By establishing these expectations up front, we were able to help one set of customers (the outside vendor) succeed in servicing another set of customers (our employees). And the employers of these service providers benefited as well. When word got out that Southwest was one of their accounts, they were able to attract great people—who, of course, wanted to work on the Southwest projects. So the vendors got great people, and then they assigned them to us. This was a win/win situation for many different people: Our employees got what they needed the way they needed it; Southwest was able to serve its customers; and vendors were able to grow successful businesses with great people.

I'd love to see this question of "Who is HR's customer?" finally put to bed once and for all. To be successful, every company must be a customer service company first. And to be a true customer service company, the enterprise must regard everyone who does business with the company—within or outside it—as a customer. The philosophy removes the divisive "us versus them" perspective.

To paraphrase Pogo: We've seen the customer, and it is us.

Building a From-the-Heart
HR Function—And a World-Class
Organization, While You're at it

CHAPTER 26

How to Make Your Company a Great Customer Service Company

Over the years, many consultants, academics, and reporters have tried to crack the code of Southwest's excellence. They've wanted to know its secret, the glowing, golden something lurking deep within its heart that makes it such an incredibly successful example of good business. I'll save you some time and tell you the answer right now. It's the passion, commitment, and extraordinary understanding of the power of customer service that makes up the DNA of the organization. The origin of this code of life is Colleen Barrett, now president and COO. Her take on customer service isn't an ordinary, run-of-the-mill customer service philosophy in which employees are encouraged to smile and say, "Have a nice day." Instead, her approach is what evolutional biologist Thomas Huxley would call "trained and organized common sense." In fact, she has been known to say many times:

"Southwest is not an airline that happens to be excellent in customer service. We're a customer service company that happens to be an airline."

Customer service is infused throughout all the functions of the company because the company created the position of executive vice president of customers more than a decade ago, when the organization began to grow exponentially. The position is among the most powerful and important in the company. As the position was originally devised, any business function that touched a person either inside or outside the organization was under that person's jurisdiction. This means people, customer relations, marketing, government affairs, corporate communications, and the frequent flyer program, among other areas.

When you consider yourself a customer service company first and foremost (to the point where the actual planes themselves become an "oh, by the way"), customer service is at the top of the business agenda. At Southwest, it concerns absolutely everyone. It's baked into all the processes and systems, starting with product development and continuing well beyond delivery.

This emphasis poses a special challenge for HR, as well as offering HR a special opportunity. If you expect employees to treat the company's external customers like gold, the first place to model that behavior is within the company itself. Therefore, the employees must know firsthand what it means to be treated with the utmost respect and consideration. That's a pretty picture, and most HR professionals would automatically say, "Sure! I get that!" But unless you're utterly and thoroughly committed to customer service as a way of life, it's a very heavy burden to be hoisting on a daily basis. When you *are* utterly and thoroughly committed to customer service as a way of life, your business takes off.

While the ideals of customer service may begin at "the table," their practical application begins with the employees. And so it's with the employees—all the employees, no matter where they are in the company—that the company demonstrates its customer service philosophy. And that makes the HR department the most influential customer service department in the company. The HR department is where the brand promise comes alive.

Make Sure You Hire the Right People to Begin With

As we've discussed already, hiring must be the entire company's core competency, and hiring decisions should be the purview of HR. (For a time, we even had passengers help us interview flight attendants.) Every single person—regardless of function—must have a strong philosophy of customer service. This is where most companies lose the customer service battle—they assume that only those employees who actually deal with customers should have that frame of reference and talent. In fact, every single person in the organization touches the customer in one way or another. No one works in a vacuum. Therefore, at Southwest, we asked every candidate for every job specific questions that were designed to reveal the candidate's people and service attitudes. If people didn't show an understanding of their connection in the customer service supply chain, they wouldn't get hired, no matter how good they were in their profession or area of expertise.

Season Every Training Class with a Customer Service Message

At the beginning of every year, we would develop a special customer service message for that year, and we would include it in every class, from technical job training to leadership development classes.

Start Your High-Potential Employees in Customer Relations or Other Positions That Require Them to Deal With Customers

When they begin their career in your company with such a position, they carry an understanding of customer needs and a sensitivity to those needs throughout their entire career. They never lose sight of the real bottom line: making the customer happy. One program that worked very well for us was to assign new employees with strong writing skills to our customer relations representative group for the first couple of years. Their job was to answer customers' letters. They didn't have form letters to resort to. They were required to thoroughly investigate the customers' complaints and concerns and find out what went wrong. By the time they were finished with this assignment, they knew every single department, how it operated, who the people in each department were, and what issues *they* faced on a daily basis. From that beginning, they could go almost anywhere in the company to continue their careers. They were a good source of recruiters for the People Department. They, of all people, knew best what would make good customer service people.

Encourage Back Office Staff and Management to Work Face to Face with Customers Occasionally

There will be employees who don't face the public as part of their daily jobs. Make sure they spend time on the front lines. At Southwest, everyone in management is required to spend one day per quarter doing work that brings them into contact with the customers. Some work behind the ticket counter; some load and unload bags; others work in the reservations center. I would spend my days working in the crew scheduling areas, behind the ticket counters, and in customer service areas to see how our *internal* customer service system was working and to spend time in the field with our people.

Those were the days when I learned the most about the job we were doing in HR. One time, while I was working behind the ticket counter in Providence, I was told that candidates were submitting their résumés and not getting a response confirming that we had received them. That couldn't be possible! Our response system was sacrosanct; everyone who wrote to Southwest about anything got some kind of response. So I checked with my department, and the people there swore that they had generated the postcards. There was a disconnect here somewhere. But where? We traced those postcards all the way to the mailroom, where we discovered that the mailroom staff was throwing them away! Apparently the postcards wouldn't go through the postage machines, so someone decided that they weren't important enough to worry about and just pitched them.

Have Knowledgeable Customers

Educate your customers as to what exactly your product is and what they can expect from you. This is especially important when your business model includes a twist in front-line operating procedures that could be a culture shock to your customers. In an industry in which the airlines typically differentiate themselves by their style and level of service, the casual and fun atmosphere of the Southwest way could be perceived as, well, *too* casual and fun. This happened to Southwest when we started service in California. We were struggling with two challenges: Competing against the higher-paying employers on the West Coast made hiring great people there tough, and we didn't enter California gradually. We blossomed into multiple locations, requiring way too many employees way too fast.

On top of that, the California customers just didn't get us at first. Open seating? No meals? To a flying public that was used to valet parking and car detailing in its airport parking lots, this level of service spelled only one thing: cattle car. We had to make the extra effort to market the message: We're not bad. We're just different. Our people are nice. Your trip will be cost-efficient and fun.

Make Customer Service Heroes out of Your Employees

I recall a time when a grown son dropped his elderly, wheelchair-bound mother off at the gate with no money, except for just a little change in her purse (can you imagine?). As Murphy's Law would have it, bad weather rolled in. All planes were canceled, completely stranding Mom at the airport. A gate agent found out about Mom's plight and personally took her to a hotel and checked her in at the agent's own expense (trusting, of course, that Southwest would reimburse her). The next morning, she checked on the passenger and made sure she made her flight. Here was a situation that was rife with potential trouble, risk, and expense for the gate agent. And it wasn't as if she was dealing with a frequent flyer who would be flying again and again and again. Still, because of the support, encouragement, and freedom Southwest gives its employees to do the right thing—regardless of cost or perceived return on investment—our agent was able to take meaningful action based on what her heart told her was *right* and not what a policy manual told her was a *must* or, worse, a *must not*.

Our passenger wrote us a wonderful letter, which we included in our Packet of Good Letters, a monthly compilation of passenger praise that we would distribute throughout the company. This monthly treat was one of the highlights of my time at Southwest.

Customer retention should be a key value for every company. Therefore, we all need employees who can take the extra step, take the extra risk, and make the necessary sacrifices to serve the customers' needs—no matter how far off the "script" they must wander to do that. Celebrate those moments as publicly as you can. That's the best way you can retain Customer Number One: the employee.

Building a From-the-Heart
HR Function—And a World-Class
Organization, While You're at it

CHAPTER 27

Eight Ways to Sell the Value of Your Department

If you look at any given company, from one-third to one-half of the costs of doing business of that company are expended on people issues. For many businesses, that's their largest single investment. Thankfully, many enlightened organizations are beginning to realize that people are an *investment* rather than a *cost* of doing business. Phrases such as "human capital," "people value management," "knowledge workers," and "intellectual capital" are cropping up in our business vernacular. However, I am not sure that we have reached the point where investments in HR as a function are viewed as producing the appropriate ROI on the dollars invested in people. We have to dedicate more of our own energies in helping others to understand more thoroughly that investing in people really does provide a very valuable return.

Historically, the people assets have been looked upon as business expenses, and the costs associated with running the HR department and HR initiatives have been seen as necessary evils, not as value drivers. This is because many HR leaders were not able to demonstrate the value that HR delivered to the organization on a regular basis, and we assumed that we really couldn't justify all of our costs. Sure, we hire, develop, and support people, and we keep the business in compliance with employment laws and regulations. If we weren't here, maybe the people wouldn't get hired (or at least the *right* people wouldn't get hired); they wouldn't get paid; they wouldn't be able to keep their skills up to date; they wouldn't be motivated; turnover would be a problem; and so on. And the company's general counsel might be paying huge sums in settlement costs as well-meaning managers were hauled into court on harassment and discrimination charges. Looking at it another way, what would it cost to outsource the hiring, the compensation planning, the employee development, and the compliance, and what effect would having these things done by outsiders have on the corporate culture? We can make the argument that while what we do may not directly generate *new* revenue for the company, we provide the company with millions of dollars in productivity gains, and we save the company millions in legal fees. After a while that adds up to some real money. A million saved is sometimes better than a million earned. But that argument isn't enough.

So why is it that we are always the first ones to have our resources reduced the minute there are corporate cutbacks? The answer is: People may be seen as an investment, but when the going gets tough, that thinking about them as an *investment* reverts to thinking about them as *expense*. Certain levels of talent may be expendable, and certain investments may be "nice to do" instead of "must haves." And what about HR itself? We don't aggressively market our accomplishments and our value to the company. We allow our activities to be discussed in terms of costs, without measuring and talking about the benefits we provide and the long-term impact of those benefits. As we've already discussed, take your lead from the advertising department and the commercials you see on television. Learn to speak in a language that goes straight to the hearts of the key decision makers—and that language includes hard numbers.

Quantify the Value of Your Department Every Chance You Get

How many of the things you do can you translate into numbers? Cost per hire is a good start. Even more compelling is turnover costs. Demonstrate in numerical terms that every time your company loses a valued employee, the ripple effect on costs extends far beyond the cost of advertising the opening, a few hours of recruiters' time, and a couple of days of lower productivity. Estimates of the costs of hiring a replacement for a key employee range from 30 percent to 200 percent of annual salary. Show numerically what happens when employees are allowed to get frustrated and choose to leave the business. One source of power is the ability to speak specifically in terms of money saved and money earned. Learn how to do that, and do it as often as you can.

Find the Key People-Measurement Gauges That Will Measure Your Contribution to the Overall Corporate Business Plan

You can focus on productivity measures by looking at data points such as revenue per employee, costs per employee, days lost through absences or injuries, increased performance levels or results, or turnover. You can implement an active cost management program by looking at HR department costs per employee, employee benefit costs, hiring costs, turnover costs, overtime costs, temporary labor costs, and so on. You can measure the effectiveness of HR programs by measuring whether or not your bonus plans are yielding the desired results, by evaluating whether your base pay plans are attracting and retaining the right candidates, or by following up with trainees to see if training yielded higher performance levels. What value does your culture contribute? How effective is the service delivered to employees and managers? The ultimate measurement would be the measurement of what HR contributes overall to business results. Can you show how your HR agenda has affected the bottom line? How do you compare with your competitors or the best companies in other industries?

Make the Business Case for Each of HR's Business Objectives

You must be able to provide senior leadership with good information about the workforce: what is working and what isn't working, where there are opportunities to increase productivity or achieve cost savings, or what investment is needed to drive the business agenda. HR must have meaningful metrics to measure the value it delivers. If HR is seen as overhead or administrative costs, we cannot obtain the resources we need if we are to improve the processes in ways that will deliver talent and technologies and add to the overall employment experience. Compare what it costs to perform administrative functions internally as opposed to outsourcing, and don't forget to include costs or the impact on culture if employees cannot get service internally.

Don't Forget Customer Feedback

When it comes to staffing, compensation and benefits, employee development, or employee service centers, what is the level of customer satisfaction? What value was delivered? What effects did the customers see? Your internal customer is an important customer, but what you do every day affects your *external* customers' experience with your company and your product. Can you measure that?

Pick the Right Metrics for Your Organizational Culture

Don't get too sophisticated and complicated if your organization isn't driven by metrics. How do your peers in marketing or finance measure their effectiveness? See if you can find parallels for HR that are meaningful to your organization. What does your finance department use to measure overall company performance? Can you copy that model somehow?

Use Language That Excites Your Colleagues

No one gets excited when you say, "I need *x* amount of dollars for employment advertising to generate applicants." To senior leadership, an applicant is a faceless, jobless wannabe, just another online résumé submitted using your résumé generation app. But if you say instead, "We need to fill the pipeline with talent that's ready to meet your needs, and I've projected that we should have x number of people in that pipeline to ensure that we'll have the best selection when we need it," that helps your audience envision their plans actually coming to pass, with the help of the best employees for the job. Make a business case for your need. And that business case must always address your company's ambitions.

It all comes down to what's important to the organization. I've seen more and more organizations say that attracting and retaining high-quality employees is one of the most important keys to building a healthy future. So start from that premise. If that's a key, it should be one of your core competencies. If it's one of your core competencies for the long term, what do the company and its HR department need to understand about the power of hiring the right people from the start?

What kinds of people will perpetuate the culture your company desires? You can hire one person low in the company who eventually rises to become CEO. Or you can hire one person in a seemingly inconsequential position who eventually brings the organization to its knees. Find the words to describe the success variables and use them frequently and intensely to promote the fact that your HR mission is integrally aligned with your company's mission-critical objectives.

Meet regularly with your constituencies and ask them, "What are the most important ways I can help you right now?" Are they getting the right kinds of hires? Are compensation and benefits working in their area? Listen carefully. Make adjustments when you can. And then tell people that you've made those adjustments.

Brand and Ballyhoo HR

Get very friendly with your corporate communications department. The people there are doing all sorts of projects that directly affect your employees anyway, so they might as well do it with your input. (You'd be amazed at how many employment branding initiatives get their start in corporate communications, bypassing HR altogether. In fact, some corporate communications departments don't even *think* of including HR in such a program. It doesn't even occur to them.)

Start internal communications initiatives that celebrate what HR is accomplishing. They have to be sincere, genuine, and issued with the right frequency—not too much, not too little. Only you and your department will know what that balance is. Try to tie your message to the external messaging to customers. Internal branding ties what you deliver to your customer with what you deliver to your employees. As discussed in Chapter 20, at Southwest our external brand was *Freedom*. And our internal brand was "Freedom begins with me."

At Yahoo! we're developing a new external corporate brand that will be based on the idea that "Yahoo! helps you get more out of the Internet." Our internal brand will send the message that we will help you get more out of your work life. But the message is going to be much more subtle than that at Southwest because people at Yahoo! are very skeptical of HR programs. So we'll keep our messaging low-key and appropriate to the culture.

Encourage Word of Mouth

Use focus groups when they're appropriate. Get people to talk to you about what's working and what's not working. At Southwest, if we really wanted to know what was going on in the real world, we asked the pilots. They saw what was happening every day across our system. Who are the "pilots" in your organization? You can use what you read on Internet message and chat boards to your advantage. I have seen the rumors and opinions expressed on message boards upset more than a few corporate officers, but I look at these messages as data. This is the same stuff that we used to hear in the break rooms and at the water cooler. The Internet message board is replacing the restroom graffiti, the bulletin board postings, and anonymous memos. I have been known to occasionally add my own comments to message boards to correct a rumor or answer a question with accurate information. You'd be amazed at how surprised employees were to see my response to their message. Exit interviews are a good source of what is working and what is not working, but, sadly, you are hearing it from those who are already voting with their feet.

Don't get defensive when you hear negative comments and observations. If the data hold value for you, summarize and communicate your findings, take the information, and use it to fix what's wrong. And then *tell people* that you've taken the necessary steps. And, of course, measure the impact of the fix.

Model the behavior you want to see take root in your company. Say good things about your colleagues and coworkers. And when someone says a kind or positive thing about you, thank that person and tell him or her how much you appreciate it.

Don't forget that the intangibles or spiritual aspects are more important than the tangibles. The level of trust in the organization, levels of employee engagement, and an employee-centered culture can be indicators of superior shareholder value. When you report on these elements, echo the words of the employees, tell stories, and show meaning . . . not just the numbers. (But remember to show the numbers, too.)

Building a From-the-Heart HR Function—And a World-Class Organization, While You're at it

CHAPTER 28

The Truth Behind Those Best Employers Lists
This Ain't No Beauty Contest!

Back in the 1980s, Robert Levering and Milton Moskowitz embarked on a marvelous project for all the right reasons. They set out to find the best employers in the United States, and they published their findings in a spectacularly popular book, *The 100 Best Companies to Work For in America*. That was a great idea, and it spawned a trend: Magazines began producing similar lists. *Fortune* magazine absorbed the team's original research and, with the early help of Hewitt Associates, has been publishing an annual list of 100 Best Employers since the late 1990s.

I'm very proud to say that Southwest made the top ten list four years running, and was even Number One in 1998, the first year the list was published. But appearance on such a list is a mixed blessing. Which leads me to a story about a young man in a lawn chair.

One morning I arrived at work early, which was unusual for me. My phone started ringing about 8:00 A.M. "Hey, Libby! Did you see the guy in the parking lot?" I went out to the parking lot and, sure enough, there was a young man out there dressed in a suit and tie (remember, this was summer in Dallas), comfortably set up in a lawn chair and holding a sign that read, "Will work for peanuts!"

After inviting him into the cool building, we naturally sent a recruiter to interview him on the spot. He said he had heard about us in college. In fact, one of our recruiters had spoken to his class. He had read everything about us that he could find and had even written papers about Southwest. And now that he had graduated from business school, he knew from everything he had read that he wanted to work for us. He had sent in résumés and filled out applications, but that had gotten him nowhere. So he had jumped into his car and driven all the way from Utah with this extraordinary strategy in mind. It worked. It got our attention. And we offered him a job. But he turned it down, saying that the salary didn't meet his expectations. We had offered him an entry-level position, rather than the management-level opportunity he had his heart set on.

One of my colleagues said afterward, "He won't really work for peanuts. He'll work for chocolate-covered macadamia nuts."

So what does the Best Employers list have to do with ambitious young men in parking lots? This young man probably wouldn't have thought twice about us as a potential employer if it hadn't been for the renown that being on that list had brought Southwest. Being famous for being a great place to work is a wonderful thing. But being on that list (and others like it) has both upsides and downsides. And one of the downsides is that it sets up expectations in the outside world that are impossible to meet. A Best Employer is not paradise. It's not Nirvana. It's not even a trip to Disney World (unless you happen to work for Disney). It's going to work day in and day out, dealing with the same kinds of people, trying to get the job done and trying to turn a profit while you're at it. Some of us just have a better time doing all that than others do.

The way we got on Levering and Moskowitz's radar in the earliest days was perhaps the best, most satisfying part of being on these lists. We didn't go after the recognition. The recognition came to us—and in the best possible way: through our reputation of doing well what was important to us. We didn't even know Levering and Moskowitz existed while they were quietly asking CEOs and HR leaders around the country: "What companies do you think are great places to work?" I'm very happy to be able to say that Southwest came up again and again.

So they came out to see us. Working off a checklist they had already prepared, they asked us about all the different factors that they had identified as being hallmarks of top employer cultures. "Do you have this benefit?" No. "Do you have that program?" No. Family benefits? No. Total Quality Management? No. Flexible work schedules? No. No, no, no. We didn't subscribe to any of these programs. We didn't think much more about it, because we hadn't gone in search of that kind of recognition from the outside world in the first place. Were we ever surprised when we made the top ten! Southwest got top billing for pay and benefits, job opportunities, job security, pride in work and company, openness and fairness, and camaraderie and friendliness.

According to the book, the biggest plus to working at Southwest is: "It's a blast to work here." And the biggest minus is: "You may work your tail off."

Later we found out how we had made it. The authors had surveyed 200 randomly chosen employees. Based on their responses, we ranked Number One in employee satisfaction, even though we didn't have any of those clever, cutting-edge plans.

Even though we didn't have any of the bells and whistles, we still eventually became The Best Company to Work For, and of course we were thrilled! We had a big celebration with our employees, and we used the news in some of our employment ads. And then we went back to work. But we noticed that some of the other companies on the list made a *really big deal* out of it, mentioning their status more and more. And that put us off the whole idea. It began to feel like a beauty contest. And even though we continued to participate each year for a while, we felt more and more that companies were competing to be *on the list*, rather than to actually be *best employers*.

Over the years we continued filling out the survey, pulling the employee data, and investing 100 or so hours in assembling what we thought the list managers needed in order to make their annual judgment. Then someone clued us in: A lot of other companies were hiring big PR firms to get them on the list. Our confidant said, "You're still filling out the forms by hand. You're not bringing us any slick presentations, special packaging, or videotapes." That wasn't what we were all about. And so eventually Southwest decided to discontinue participating in the program. Which was fine.

To be fair, there are still some wonderful benefits associated with being on these lists. You and your employees experience a true sense of pride when you know you're working for a company that has been recognized in this way. Your friends say, "Aren't you lucky to be working for a best employer!" Even your customers are proud to be associated with a company that treats its employees well. (When I'm a passenger on a plane, I like knowing that the people who are responsible for my comfort and safety like their jobs.) And you begin to add to the body of knowledge surrounding excellence in HR. Consultants and professors want to start researching your company. You become the subject of studies and white papers and articles. You become legendary. And you attract dedicated, ambitious new candidates to your company—which is really great if you have a strong philosophy of hiring at entry levels and promoting from within (which is the one minor, but important, detail that our work-for-peanuts guy hadn't quite absorbed before he input his driving directions from Utah to Texas into Yahoo! Maps).

That's one of the downsides of these lists. The Southwest way may not be so great if you're an ambitious new grad who's hoping to start making your dreams come true right away and having a fast upward climb. Those lists promote unrealistic expectations among the community of potential employees and current employees, who come to expect more than your company can provide.

Once you get on one list, other publishers of lists want you to participate in theirs. It's wonderful to be known as a best employer for working mothers, for women, for minorities, for seniors, for every other group that is looking for a welcoming place to make its dreams come true through making the company successful. But where do you stop? What magazine do you want to say no to? Whose feelings do you choose to hurt when you finally put your foot down?

Be a best employer. But be one for the right reasons, not as a public relations tool. It is much more important to create an energizing and dynamic workplace, to have a culture that drives desired results, than it is to be on a list. Be careful if you decide to jump on the Best Employer bandwagon. You may be more successful than you want to be.

Building a From-the-Heart
HR Function—And a World-Class
Organization, While You're at it

CHAPTER 29

Congratulations!
You May Have Already Won!

You don't have to be on a Best Employers List to *be* a best employer. If beauty pageants aren't important to you, but substantive and meaningful HR contributions are, you can have all the advantages of the Best Employers campaigns without actually going through the trouble and expense of participating in them.

It can be cheap, easy, and fun. And you get the most lasting, real value for your efforts: You are known in your community and industry as one of the best companies that magnetize top performers. And you don't ever have to worry about the embarrassment that comes from losing your place on the more publicized list. You are your own list, and you can keep your place on that one as long as being a best employer is important to you.

The bad news is that you don't get to hang a banner outside your windows. But, hey, that's just window dressing anyway. Like everything else in this world that matters, it's what you have going on *inside* that counts. So what's going on inside your company?

While we were working on Southwest Airlines' submission to the *Fortune* list, we were also coincidentally working on other projects with Hewitt Associates, which did all the tabulating and analyzing of the results in the first few years the list was published. They were nice enough to share with us what they found to be common characteristics among those who made the top twenty-five on the list. They gave me permission to share with you the overall characteristics of officially recognized best employers—both general company characteristics and characteristics of their HR programs and policies. Here's what they found:

The best companies . . .

- Are always the ones that demonstrate through word and deed that each individual employee is highly and equally valued.*

- Have a high degree of employee involvement.

- Have a culture that values the individualism of others, respecting the need for people to be themselves.*

- Have very little hierarchy, distinctions, elitism, and bureaucracy.

- Have practices and programs that reflect equal, consistent, and employee-oriented policies throughout all locations and groups.*

- Provide their employees with significant opportunities to develop, grow, and learn, both professionally and personally.

- Recognize that quality-of-life issues for their employees are important components of the business agenda.

The best HR culture . . .

- Emphasizes ethical business practices, corporate caring, open work environments, strong leaders, an atmosphere of trust, and meaningful work.

*These characteristics, by the way, are key to preventing serious, companywide diversity problems. When everyone feels equally valued, you don't have as many diversity issues. Diversity issues come up when employees think that someone is routinely being favored over someone else.

- Recognizes that hiring must be a best practice and a shared responsibility among HR, line managers, and peers.

- Hires for attitude and motivation over skills and résumé.

- Focuses on culture in new hire orientation programs, equipping new employees with the necessary understanding and insight to fit into their new culture

- Emphasizes a lot of employee communication, formal and informal, in a variety of media. And repeated, again and again. Even the business plans are shared with the employees, to the extent possible under SEC regulations.

- Makes sure the communication pipeline flows both ways, with employee opinion surveys, focus groups, and reassurance to employees that their letters and emails are read and taken very seriously.

- Has a dependable complaint resolution process in place.

- Promotes a team-based culture.

- Allows decisions to be made at the lowest possible levels and involves all levels in the process of implementing change.

- Makes sure that social events and celebrations are a way of life.

- Contains formal and informal recognition programs.

- Recognizes and announces individual achievements in employee communications tools.

- Places a high value on formal performance reviews, often including 360-degree feedback.

- Bases pay on the person and the accomplishments, not the job.

- Features innovative benefit plans and perks.

- Focuses on creating a friendly place to work, where employees feel welcome and are given the tools and resources they need to do their job, and where they know that their personal success and the company's success are inextricably linked.

Innovative benefit plans and perks include:

- On-site child care

- Backup child care

- Flexible work schedules

- Health insurance for any member of the household

- New fathers paid benefits

- Medical twenty-four-hour hotline

- Free or discounted child care

- Paid family care time off

- No-cost benefits for employees and dependents

- Outdoor walking trail

- Health club facility

- Newlywed paid leave

- Massages

- Sabbatical for life-threatening illness

- Convenient parking for pregnant women

- Take-home meals

And job-related perks include:

- Computer purchase program

- Trip for veterans with twenty years' service

- Gain-sharing payments for service improvements

- On-the-spot cash rewards

- Stock options for everybody

- Retention awards in stock

- Stock purchase plan

- Bonus plans

- Clothing allowance

- Company vacation facilities

- Free lunch

- Charity/community involvement

Southwest Airlines, which placed first, second, and fourth (twice) in the list during my tenure there, had very few of these benefits and perks. We made the list by valuing our people and their contributions and by creating a very satisfying culture and opportunities. So before you invest in that Olympic-sized pool or a cabin in the woods, check out your leadership team, your culture, and how people feel about their work and the organization.

CHAPTER 30

Show Them the Money!

Back in the early 1990s, I was generally suspected by business experts and compensation gurus of sitting on a big secret, one the size of the Rosetta stone, the fountain of youth, and the lost Aztec gold mines all rolled into one. Even worse, I wasn't sharing it with the rest of the class. Here's why I was attracting all this attention from the media, from academics, and from fellow compensation specialists: At one of those cyclical times when the airline industry was falling apart, Southwest was happily flying in the black. At a time when it had become fashionable for the flying public to bemoan the good old days of air travel, when it was still special and people got dressed up for their flights (and when, by the way, hardly anyone could afford it), that little unpretentious airline from Texas was setting customer service, on-time performance, and baggage handling records. And, to top it all off, we were doing all this at a profit—when the other airlines were hemorrhaging cash.

Well, clearly something was going on over there at Love Field. And clearly, since all of Southwest's outstanding performance was people-driven, there must be some mighty mojo happening in the People

Department. So it only stood to reason that Libby must be hanging on to a miracle compensation formula that was extracting insanely great results from people who were, as it was generally understood, underpaid in comparison to employees at the other airlines. What could be my secret? And why wouldn't I give it up?

Finally the American Compensation Association (ACA), now WorldatWork, prevailed upon me to write an article for its scholarly journal about how Southwest's marvelous compensation program fosters such world-class customer service. No matter how hard I protested, saying, "You aren't going to like what I have to say," the editor was sure that once the article was written, all would be revealed. The article I wrote was entitled "Culture Drives Southwest's Performance, Not Compensation." For those who subscribe to standards of compensation theory and practice, the article was close to blasphemy. But, while the ACA eventually determined that the article wasn't quite right for the journal, it did find its way into the association's member newspaper.

Here is the basic principle: If you look at compensation only as a *plan*, you're missing more than half the story. Your total compensation program must be informed not by a plan but by a *philosophy*. And Southwest knew how to leverage its philosophy to make it a stand-out performer in an industry bound by utterly restrictive and completely uninspiring pay rules, as negotiated in nine separate collective bargaining agreements that determined how 85 percent of our employees (the industrious and the lazy alike) would be paid. Whether you were beginning work as a new high school grad or you had been in the field for thirty years, only one thing determined your salary: time on the job. You couldn't outshine or outperform your way to bigger paychecks. Your colleagues at other airlines—those who hadn't yet been laid off, at least—might be living higher off the proverbial hog with slightly higher take-home pay. What could possibly motivate these people to do so well that they kept Southwest not just flying but soaring?

The motivating differentiator was simply this: Herb Kelleher's compensation philosophy. Material rewards are important—but only up to a point. They quickly become hollow unless they are accompanied by psychic satisfaction. And that psychic satisfaction entails pride in one's work (along with the culture of mutual respect), fulfillment, and fun. When you have those elements in place, you can motivate people to do almost anything you could possibly want them to do.

This philosophy significantly simplifies any compensation and benefits plan. It makes your own job more rewarding. But it is also hugely demanding. You can never fall back on the seemingly simple solution of throwing money at the problem. And, although you recognize that compensation is a major cost of doing business, you must also view it as not just a tool, but an investment that will pay off if properly managed. You have to be fully engaged, authentic, and creative every single moment. This philosophy will also be the secret of your success, and it will drive your competitors crazy as they try to crack the code. Unfortunately (for them), they're more likely to try to crack the code by . . . that's right, throwing more money at their compensation challenges.

Most organizations think that paying what they have to pay in order to get the skills and talents they need will solve their problems. True, they may get the skills and talents they need, but they will not necessarily be able to *keep* these employees, or even fully engage them while they are on the payroll. By dangling money as the sole carrot, employers attract the kinds of employees who are most motivated by money. And that appeal wears off very quickly. So every time you meet a requested or expected price, that amount will never be enough for long.

In fact, the traditional compensation plan is merely an extrinsic reward that can't truly affect the way someone feels about his or her job (although it can produce a negative feeling if the employee feels significantly underpaid). The best compensation plan in the world can't make people love a job that isn't a good fit for them or one that they hate doing. It can't make them overlook a terrible boss, terrible leadership, or an industry that they despise. It can't make them happy (at least, not for long), no matter how hard you try. You have to be able to offer employees a reward for their efforts that is longer-lasting and more intrinsically meaningful.

There are other elements of the compensation *philosophy* that will support the *plan* and drive truly high performance over the long term, regardless of the economy. These elements include intrinsic and intangible variables, such as a respectful and mission-driven culture, great leadership, and a corporate cause that employees can relate to on a deeply personal level. Your compensation philosophy (and the related plan) should foster a sense of ownership among all the employees throughout the company, at all its locations.

I once heard a wonderful story about a Southwest gate operations agent who was facing a crammed terminal full of passengers stuck in a heavy Texas summer storm, with grounded planes backed up awaiting their turn at six gates. The place was a madhouse. She stood on a chair so that everyone could see her and announced, "Ladies and gentlemen, I need everyone's attention! I have an airline to run and these are my flights! And I'm going to get you out of here!"

This person knew in her heart that Southwest belongs to her. Yes, part of that commitment comes from having stock in the company. But mostly it comes from the way senior leadership communicates to all Southwest employees every day that sense of empowerment and responsibility to make the difference.

The basic tool for this kind of communication is, indeed, compensation. But no amount of cash in this person's paycheck would have compelled her to jump on a chair and take charge. The real currency that binds people to their companies is from-the-heart respect and communications that give them what they need to do their jobs, to do them well, and then to be sincerely recognized, rewarded, and sometimes just plain thanked for their hard work.

That is the secret foundation of any from-the-heart compensation philosophy.

CHAPTER 31

Using Benefits to Build Relationships

"So tell me about yourself." That's an interview moment that leaves many candidates stammering and struggling for something great to say. But smart interviewees recognize that request as an opportunity to set themselves off from the crowd of highly credentialed and qualified candidates. Everything else being equal, the way they describe themselves can add competitive differentiating details that make them the winner. It's a creative opportunity for them to make a stand and to state what their values are, what they believe in, how they envision the future, and what steps they're taking to make that future happen.

Your company's benefits plan does the same thing—it's a competitive differentiating factor that goes far beyond its traditional role of providing the "fringe" considerations that were once special but that we now take for granted as entitlements; paid sick and vacation leave and health-care benefits are common examples. Your benefits plan is a creative and dynamic opportunity to demonstrate in real and meaningful ways exactly what your company's values and beliefs are, what its vision for the future is, and what steps you're taking to make that future happen. More than ever before, your benefits program—what it contains and how it's administered—is your chance to set your company apart from the pack. Is the benefits program saying the right things about your company?

Take Off Your Hat and Stay a While

Companies with barely adequate benefits programs aren't establishing a relationship of mutual partnering in which the company and the individual employees help each other realize their long-term objectives. Those companies that really want employees to be engaged for a couple of years at best have benefits plans that send out the message: "Just please stay healthy while you're on our time, will you?" Only basic health-care coverage is offered, and high copayments, high deductibles, or other low-cost participation structures help the companies keep their costs down and the employees functioning in the short term. Plans that don't emphasize or reward preventive health care signal to the employees that their long-term interests are of no special concern to the company. And that's fine, especially for a company in a start-up mode where most people don't expect long-term security, as long as everyone is clear on this point. Just remember that most employees take their long-term health prospects (and the health of their families) rather personally, and eventually this could be the deciding factor in their departure.

Companies that want to encourage long-term relationships with their employees do everything they can to help them build futures that count. This means not only comprehensive and easily affordable health care, but opportunities to build financial security, opportunities to provide for retirement income, and benefits that support diverse families and lifestyles. These benefits say that we want to try to provide for the needs of all kinds of employees. To get the most bang for your benefits buck, benefits must be well communicated and understood and must be tied to the culture of the organization. At the best companies, employees are offered the choice of covering their families and partners; health, wellness, and recreation are emphasized; work/life benefits are there for families; flexible work arrangements are sponsored; and there is paid time off when needed. While approaches to financial security vary, these companies offer retirement income, savings, life insurance, long-term disability insurance, financial education and counseling, and stock plans. This is more than traditional benefits packages offer, but in addition employees are offered meaningful help in cultivating their personal prospects through additional educational opportunities and career advancement. Offering tuition reimbursement, company-sponsored training and development, e-learning opportunities, seminars, certification courses, discreet adult literacy courses, and English as a Second Language courses and partnering with local community colleges to provide ongoing skills training show people that you are committed to their future career growth, even though there is a risk that additional education will also prepare people for jobs at other companies.

Wow!!

For the most part, companies must provide a certain level of benefits in order to compete in the job market. To provide signature benefits, those that really "wow" your employees and prospects, takes commitment, effort, and expense.

At Southwest, the Wow element was profit sharing. Southwest sponsors the oldest and most generous profit-sharing plan in the airline industry. The plan is designed to accumulate retirement savings for employees while enabling them to share in the profits of the company. The company contributes to the plan up to 15 percent of the operating profit for the year, as determined by the board of directors, in cash or common stock or a combination of both. Profit sharing is a way of life at Southwest Airlines. The plan, which became effective January 1, 1973, drives much of the spirit of keeping costs low at Southwest Airlines. Everyone shares on the basis of his or her earnings and the company's profits. Those who work more hours or fly extra trips receive a larger piece of the profit-sharing pie. Employees who participate in the plan take genuine pride in knowing that their efforts toward the profitable operation of the company may result in a sizable financial accumulation for them and increase their future financial security.

While employees may direct their investments in the plan into multiple investment accounts, many place at least some of their profit-sharing money in company stock. When the stock performs well, everyone does well. Long-term employees have retired as millionaires. Senior employees can be overheard explaining to new hires on a daily basis how waste, carelessness, and lack of hard work affect their profit sharing. Profit sharing has created peer pressure to hold costs down and to work together as a team. Commitment to the company is strong, and devotion to one another and to the customer is important. Southwest's benefits are designed for the long-term career-minded employee and support the culture.

At Yahoo! there are many Wows, such as free health care for employees and their families, health facilities or health club memberships, and free coffee bars. At our Silicon Valley headquarters, Yahoos can have their car washed, shop for birthday gifts, send flowers, drop off dry cleaning and laundry, have their film developed, and eat three low-cost meals a day. Many of these amenities and benefits were designed for "now" and are short-term rather than for the future. So, now that we are a dot-com survivor, our future benefits philosophy and offerings will be directed more toward longer-term career growth and retention. Your Wow factor is dependent on your culture and your budget, and on the way you want to differentiate your company from all the others that are competing for your talent.

CHAPTER 32

Recognition, Rewards, Fun:
The Triple Crown of
Employee Engagement

The irony is so exquisite that it's almost Zen-like. In fact, Little Grasshopper, you must be truly ready for this secret, because if it is misused, it can destroy what you're trying to create, rather than build it up.

The most powerful tool you have for creating an enlivened, dedicated, mission-driven organization of impassioned people is a tool you can't use. You can only hold it, show it to others, gently encourage others to use it, and demonstrate it every chance you get. It's a tool whose power grows only when *other* people willingly use it after being inspired by your example. *That* is where your power lies. The tool? It's the breath of life in Herb Kelleher's formula for psychic satisfaction. It's OTJJ—On The Job Joy. Its components are recognition, rewards, and fun. And when they're applied together, they can be more powerful as a motivator than even compensation.

The problem for you is that you can only set the stage for it. You can't force it. But once you choose to use it, you can turn a dreary workplace into a self-perpetuating passion machine. Are you up to that challenge?

Taken as a group, recognition, rewards, and fun are best treated as a philosophy rather than a program. Supporting and celebrating the passion and spirit of your employees must be a natural, spontaneous, and authentic part of your corporate way of life. Otherwise you will lose the foundation of trust and communication that you've already built. Your philosophy must be appropriate to the culture of your own environment. Don't try to be another Southwest Airlines. If your corporate culture is closer to that of a monastery than to that of Graceland, you can still use the principles of recognition, rewards, and fun. Just be honest. Just be from the heart.

Recognition

Simply put, the habit of recognition is the habit of letting employees know that the company sincerely values what they do. The biweekly paycheck and the accompanying benefits program go a long way in keeping people on the job, of course, but a culture that promotes sincere recognition is key to keeping those people really engaged in what they're doing. And, when it's correctly applied, recognition can be the least expensive of all your engagement initiatives. The cost is just the time it takes to sincerely pat someone on the back and say, "Thank you."

Recognition programs can be as elaborate as you want them to be. But unless they have a core of sincere appreciation, they will come across as contrived, hollow, and even manipulative—thus turning your good intentions against you. Recognition must also be delivered in the form that is most meaningful to the individual employees. Some people deeply appreciate a quiet, discreet, one-on-one moment. Others relish a public display of gratitude and celebration. Still others are actually embarrassed if you make a big deal of their accomplishments.

At Southwest we had business-card-size cards with little sentiments printed on them, such as "You did a fantastic job!" or "You are awesome!" They were little, trivial expressions of appreciation—sort of like those hard-candy Valentine hearts that come out every year.

People would hand them out to coworkers at appropriate moments. When the idea of distributing them came up in a culture committee meeting, I secretly thought, "That's so stupid." But because the others liked the idea, I didn't object. Much to my amazement, the cards became an important part of our culture of recognition, and they were a big deal to people who received them from their coworkers. Before long, people had them tacked up all over their cubicles. I even got a few myself. And I would sincerely think, "How nice," stick them in my desk drawer, and quickly forget about them.

What meant the world to me as an employee at Southwest? I have a very small collection of handwritten notes thanking me for doing a good job on this project or that one. I don't remember the dollar amount of bonuses or percentage increase of raises I may have gotten at the time I received those notes. But I'll never forget the notes, because I cherish them. I will never throw them away.

Rewards

Sometimes your appreciation needs to take a more tangible (and perhaps more valuable) form than a simple thank you. We're used to regarding raises—especially merit increases—as rewards for performance. But if we depended exclusively on that tool, either our rewards program would get really, really expensive really, really quickly or the opportunities to give tangibly valuable thanks would be very, very limited. Even when money is being spent, imagination combined with sincerity can take you a long way.

On-the-spot recognition programs are an obvious favorite. Nothing beats looking up from your computer to see your boss standing there with a check in her hand. Does it matter how much the check is for? Well, the more the merrier, obviously. But whether the check is for $2,000 or $20, the gratitude impact is the same.

A gift also makes a wonderful recognition tool, as long as it's appropriate to both the company giving it and the person receiving it. But this requires a little thought—and that can be bad news if you're looking for easy answers. The gift has to be appropriate not only to the person but also to the organization providing the gift. A friend of mine who worked at a health-care software company went to a week-long new hire orientation training program. And, as at most of these adult-learning events, little trinkets were given out to reward correct answers, participation, and so on. By the time he was done with the week, he had quite a collection of miniature Walt Disney characters. What, I asked him, did Mickey Mouse have to do with health-care software? His answer: "Beats me."

Then it dawned on me: The person running this program had probably attended a Disney Institute leadership training program, and the Disney trainer had used Disney tchotchkes to keep the class lively. It seemed like a good idea in Orlando. It should be able to play in Dallas. There was only one problem: The company was a software maker for hospitals, not Disney!

When you give out any kind of tangible reward, make sure it reinforces the culture and values of your company, not of someone else's. All sorts of items can carry your company's logo: coffee mugs, flip-flops, koozies, coasters, cameras, T-shirts, gym bags. If you're running a health-care software company training program, fling out packets of cough drops, perhaps specially packaged in a logo'd wrapping. Give away thermometers or the dreaded height/weight chart. Use your imagination. Make it fun! Make it appropriate!

Also make it appropriate to the recipient. If a more thoughtful reward is called for, think about what the person would like. Some people like plaques. Others would appreciate the chance to have lunch with you one-on-one. If your employee plays golf, give her a half-day off to play a round at a special course near you. Or, if your budget is more limited (or you're not *that* grateful), a box of top-quality golf balls speaks volumes. The thought you invest in creating the perfect reward is just as valuable as the reward itself. It tells your employees that you know them as individuals and that you celebrate their uniqueness. It really is the thought that counts.

Fun

Fun and rewards are closely related in that they infuse your corporate culture with the joy of working at your company. But they're different in one important way: Rewards celebrate individual achievement, and fun is a communal "happening." Fun is for, by, and about everyone in the company. Again, it must be spontaneous, genuine, from the heart, and real. It must also be as all-inclusive as possible, leaving no one out and inviting all your employees to be themselves.

But that doesn't mean it can't be planned. As I write this, I'm still recovering from my first Yahoo! summer picnic, in which I participated in the dunking booth (guess which end of the transaction I was on). At Southwest, of course, we had many employee parties and picnics. But we weren't rigidly committed to the traditional barbecue and badminton scenario. One summer it was so hot that we couldn't stand the idea of going outside for anything other than running for our air-conditioned cars. One of the employees in the People Department got the brainy idea of having an indoor picnic. We brought the blankets, the barbecue, and the watermelon (of course, this was the HR department!), and we all sat on the floor of our cool offices. Among the umpteen chili cook-offs, barbecues, and summer picnics we had at Southwest while I was there, that was the picnic I will never forget.

Halloween was the holiday that presented the most opportunities for fun at Southwest. Since the People Department was genetically horrible at decorations, we made it our business to make a spectacle of *ourselves*, producing a show every year with progressively worse songs. The first year started off modestly with a rewritten version of the *Gilligan's Island* theme song. But then we had a choir of singing nuns (that was the year *Sister Act* was in the theaters) with a fake preacher delivering the Southwest "religion." Our song that year was "I Will Follow Herb." That was the year, I'm proud to say, we won the first ever "Highly Effective and Most Obvious Suck-Up to Herb Award." Following up that year were performances of the Southwest Side Story, Rock 'n' Roll Hall of Fame, Herbie Awards, and Herb's Finger (after Goldfinger). We easily won the annual award six years running.

If your company doesn't already have a culture of fun, you may feel as if you're starting out flat-footed. How do you infuse whimsy when your company is staffed by a collection of sobersides? As gently as possible. It's easy to get a culture of fun started, but it has to be introduced gradually. Start by celebrating the completion of a huge project or a win. Celebrate those big accomplishments, and take the time to do it when they happen. Don't wait until your calendar opens up before you allow yourself to take the time away from the grindstone. It never will. And after enough time passes, the achievement will feel like old news and you won't get around to it.

Grab the moment. Grab your coworkers. Grab the phone and order a pizza. Start small, demonstrate it, don't force it, and the rest will come naturally.

After all, who can resist joy?

The Little Things Make the Biggest Difference

Organizations spend time and money on many programs but fail to notice that it's often the little things that make the biggest difference. Showing that you care on a daily basis is the best leadership and motivational tool available, and it's also the cheapest. It's personal, and it involves one-on-one, face-to-face relationships. So it does take some effort and imagination. But the return is immeasurable.

- Send cards marking personal events and concerns, such as birthdays, sympathy, etc.

- Write a handwritten note commending the person.

- Be there and be visible. Wander around, get to know people, eat in the cafeteria, attend company events, sit in the break room, say hello in the hallway, put your desk by the coffee room.

- Get to know the *whole* person, not just what he or she represents to the company. Learn about the person's family, friends, hopes, and dreams.

- Say thank you.

- Be polite.

- Encourage people to achieve their career aspirations, even if they leave your organization to do it.

■ Deliver tough messages when necessary. But do it kindly.

■ Listen to ideas and respond with a *yes* or a *no* and a *why*.

■ Give people a pat on the back.

■ Believe that ordinary people can achieve extraordinary results.

■ Send flowers not just to employees but to their family members when appropriate.

■ Attend funerals and weddings. Funerals are the most important.

■ Laugh a lot, especially at yourself.

■ Create heroes every day.

■ Loosen up.

■ Rely on e-mail and voice mail less and talk to people face to face more.

■ Be a mentor.

■ Tell the truth.

■ Take risks.

■ Tell stories.

■ Hold meetings in fun places.

The Best Reward I Ever Received

Of all the rewarding experiences I had during my time at Southwest, this one stands out as the best. A few years ago, we had a near disaster at the company. A pilot who was attempting to land at the airport in Burbank, California, discovered that part of his landing gear would not come down. After several attempts to fix the problem, it was decided that he would make an emergency landing at Ontario International Airport (the one in southern California, not Canada), since it was less congested and had better runways. The company began the process of emergency planning that we had practiced many times. It was about 5:00 in the afternoon, and I was being interviewed by a reporter for *Fast Company* magazine, so I was clueless as to what had been going on. When the reporter left my office, my assistant was acting really strange. I told her I was going to take the reporter on a tour of the building. Her response was, "No, you have an emergency meeting and he has to leave."

Our executive team and top operations group gathered in our dispatch area, where they could talk with the pilots and discuss the landing procedure. After what seemed to be an excruciatingly long period of discussion and preparations, our pilots landed the plane smoothly on two gears. Except for maybe a sprained ankle or two from evacuating the plane via the emergency slide, no one was injured.

My favorite part of the story happened a couple of weeks later. Roger Way, the captain of that flight, showed up at company headquarters asking if he could talk to someone in customer relations. He had a lot of thank-you notes to write to everyone from air traffic controllers to emergency personnel. He joked that he could fly airplanes, but thank-you notes were a little difficult for him. Luckily, one of our sharp public relations folks met him in the hallway and escorted him to customer relations, where he got help with his letters.

Coincidentally, the public relations person also knew that our executive planning committee was in an all-day meeting in the boardroom. He walked right in, interrupting the meeting of the top company executives, and told them that Captain Way was in the building. Instead of reprimanding him for interrupting such an important meeting, they quickly devised a last-minute recognition celebration. They got on the phone and e-mail and told all employees to come out to the lobby. When Captain Way emerged from customer relations, he saw hundreds of people waiting, applauding, and singing his praises. Herb made an impromptu speech talking about the extraordinary efforts that the pilot and his first officer had made to save the day, if not the lives of the more than 120 passengers and crew members on board.

What Captain Way then said sent chills down my spine, and I'll never forget it: "I am really not a hero today. I don't know why I am getting the credit for saving lives. Let me tell you who really saved the lives of those passengers and crew. It was the People Department, which sets very high standards for hiring, and that's why we have the best pilots in the industry (and the best safety record). It is the flight training department who puts us through training twice a year. They throw every potential emergency at us. There is not a pilot at Southwest who couldn't have done exactly what I did. It was the maintenance people and the flight operations support staff who were on the radio answering my questions, telling me everything they knew about the landing gear and how to land under those conditions. And it was the executives who were there supporting me. I had the CEO, COO, executive vice president for customer service, vice president for operations, vice president for flight operations, and more talking to me, and believing I could do the job. "

That was my best day at Southwest because it validated everything we did in the People Department and everything our leadership team did every day. It said to me loud and clear, "What you do really does make a difference."

CHAPTER 33

Managing Expectations

● ●

A few months ago, one of my best employees, a woman in her mid-twenties, came to me and told me that she was going to resign. I couldn't have been more surprised. I thought she was happy with her work. Oh, she was! Was she satisfied with her compensation? Sure. Her benefits? Yes, yes, no problem. Her boss? Great boss! Her opportunities to grow? Absolutely, great future prospects.

So what could possibly be the problem? No problem at all. It was just that her best friend was getting married, and she wanted to be free to take part in the wedding festivities. Well, if that was the issue, I assured her, we could work something out—maybe an advance on her vacation time so that she could make the wedding, plus a party or two. No, you don't understand, she said. "I want to go to *all* the parties. And, there are a few more weddings. And I want to travel. And I want to just take the summer off and have some fun." I suspected that her plan was to cash in her stock options, spend down the proceeds, and then move in with her parents to figure out her next step.

Well, that was a new one on me. I had arrived in Silicon Valley after the legendary dot-com bubble had popped, and my overall feeling was that employees here were generally wise to the fact that (at least for the time being) the cutthroat competition for their time and talents had come to an end. In a matter of a few short months, the Silicon Valley area had gone from having the best employment rate in the nation to having the country's worst unemployment. Could it be that she was the last person in the Valley who hadn't heard the news? Or could it be something else? A sense of fatalism, perhaps? A new shift in expectations both for her current work and for building a future profession? Perhaps all of the above. One thing was for sure: The relative certainty of a regular paycheck in uncertain times wasn't enough to keep her.

No matter where we live, we've all seen this philosophy, either on a T-shirt or on a bumper sticker somewhere: "Life's uncertain; eat dessert first." In earlier times, when we as a nation were not required to be as thoughtful as we are now, that expression was a mildly annoying mix of American self-indulgence and typical sardonic American humor. But it's possible that we're entering a new era in which American employees are taking the position that the "now" is all that we can really know for sure. And even the "now" can change drastically in an instant. It did on September 11, and it hasn't stopped changing. From terrorism to anthrax to the economy to corporate corruption to the high-powered shooting of innocent people as they pump gas into their cars, the major news headlines have been about things that have directly affected the workplace. Consequently, people are taking a fresh look at their own personal ROI when it comes to the dedication they give to their work and careers. Whether what might happen is an out-of-the-blue plane crash or an out-of-the-blue layoff announcement, employees who have a clue may be deciding that they should take care of their immediate quality-of-life needs now and let the future take care of itself. What this means to employers is more aggressive and diverse sets of demands that seem to be entirely unrelated to the ups and downs of the job market and the economy.

It's too simplistic to say that we're in extraordinarily uncertain times. Every generation has dealt with hair-trigger life/death, hire/fire insecurities. Layoffs are not a new phenomenon. And the so-called employment contract of the 1950s and the 1960s was never as airtight as in retrospect we'd like to think it was. What's different today is that more employees than ever before are exposed to the vagaries of corporate management. Consequently, more employees are wise to the fact that they are truly captains of their own career ship—there's truly no depending on anyone other than themselves and their own wits for their long-term prospects. Consequently, as HR professionals, we have to work harder to discover and offer meaningful ways of engaging our best and brightest and keeping them engaged. And part of the challenge entails truly understanding the diverse set of expectations held by employees with different cultures in any company of any size.

Employees in their mid-forties to mid-sixties (or even older) entered the workplace at a time when it was common to hear, "Just be glad you have a job." This group was the last to even think in terms of cradle-to-grave employment with a single company and the first to realize that maybe it might not be so after all. Speaking in the most general terms, people in this group typically take a long-term perspective on their careers with their companies, on the premise that the intangible investment of time and dedication is likely to result in rewards and more desirable opportunities later. The pre-baby boomers remember the lasting psychological effects that the Depression and war rationing had on their parents and older siblings. The baby boomers went through the 1960s, the Vietnam war, the anti-establishment messages, and the disillusionment brought on by Watergate. And the late baby boomers struggled to start their careers in the terrible economic times that hit during every single presidential administration from the Carter administration forward. And while people in this group are no strangers to layoffs and shocking news headlines, their work ethic was largely formed by their parents and by an expectation of the long-term durability of the economy. By and large, a single headline was never as likely to throw them out of work as it is now. However, the headlines of today are more likely to threaten their retirement accounts, keeping them on the job longer than they had planned. If you have this group represented in your company, you have a cadre of employees who are probably thinking, "I could have cashed out and retired a couple of years ago. Now it looks like I'll be working another fifteen years just to get back to where I was before."

This group is going to have an entirely different set of expectations from its younger Generation X and Generation Y counterparts. These younger groups entered the workplace with no delusions of so-called employment security. Just as they had watched an unprecedented number of their parents and their friends' parents get divorced, they had also watched an unprecedented number of their parents and their friends' parents lose their jobs for one reason or another. They were encouraged to develop the entrepreneurial understanding that as long as they were able to add value to their organization, they could reasonably expect to be employed—as long as the organization that employed them was able to add value to its marketplace. We encouraged this group to be sharp, savvy, and smart, and to build their own skill sets based on market need. We also encouraged them—especially in the so-called New Economy—to understand that there are no promises and no guarantees. But they were also lavishly rewarded with economic prospects that had never before been available to such a large group. Given the availability of huge salaries and stock options, there were plenty of seemingly good risks to take. Consequently, even with its down employment market, Silicon Valley still has many baby millionaires driving cars that cost many times the equivalent of my father's salary.

As a result of all these generations and backgrounds working shoulder to shoulder with one another in today's workplace, we're dealing with a bouillabaisse of many, many different sets of expectations, values, and definitions of what a respectable work ethic is. And it's up to HR leadership to work it out so that the company continues to attract and hang onto the best possible talent.

■ *Understand the culture of expectations in the context of your industry or geographic area.* It takes a long time to build a major airline brand in Dallas, Texas. Consequently, the risk/investment/reward horizon at Southwest has always been in the relatively distant future. And so Southwest employees work in a culture that encourages dedication now for accrued return on their investment in the long term. In Silicon Valley, a start-up company such as Yahoo! can appear on the scene and blossom almost overnight into a huge company with offices all over the world. Everything is fast; expectations on both sides—management and employees—are high. In Silicon Valley there was an almost decade-long tradition of aggressive recruitment of the best and the brightest, and employees have grown accustomed to being rewarded for every atom of value added that they bring to the workplace.

■ *Adjust your own expectations accordingly.* The employment contract is dead. There is more of a short-term commitment now, and we've developed a "what's in it for me" culture that I still find shocking when I run up against it. It's a short-term, project-oriented, "Free Agent Nation" culture that emphasizes the sure-thing trade over the long-term investment. Is this a bad development? Or is it a good development? Probably neither, but it is definitely a natural by-product of the "no guarantees, job-for-now" employment relationship that we've developed over the last fifteen years. Not only do we have to adjust our offerings to match our employees' diverse and utterly transformed set of expectations, but we also have to adjust our own personal reactions to those demands. This one is still a challenge for me personally. As I was developing my own work ethic, I saw every opportunity to volunteer for special projects and every assignment I was given as an intangible—but very valuable benefit; a chance to learn new things, meet new people, and have career-building experiences that could benefit me in the long run. In addition, these projects were good for the company, and I wanted to be part of growing the business.

But in Silicon Valley, the culture is highly competitive, and employees have learned over the years to be equally aggressive in their negotiating positions. In an environment in which even time is a precious, marketable commodity, these people have come to regard every moment that they spend focused on their work as value added to their company, and they want to be compensated accordingly.

■ *Help your employees manage their own expectations.* Even Silicon Valley employees are experiencing a shift in their hopes for their careers and their future. But there may be times when only their own market research will convince employees that their expectations may not be consistent with reality. It's rare, but it still happens that I am approached by one of our more talented employees who thinks he should be making half a million dollars, be getting more stock options, and have a fancier title. Well, that might have been possible in the late 1990s, but it certainly isn't now. So my invitation to these people is simply this: Explore the job market. Try to get an offer like the package you want from us, but be sure to factor in the culture, the long-term growth opportunities, and the fun factor. If you find that there's a big market and demand for your abilities, let me know. I sincerely do want to know. And if you find that our package isn't so bad after all, I'd like to know that too. If employees are motivated enough to ask you for such significant increases or other cushy considerations, let them be the ones to do the market research. Once they do their own reality checks, chances are that they will withdraw their demands.

I wish my young employee who quit to go to her friend's wedding had conducted her own reality check before making such a big career decision. I valued her contribution, and it's quite possible that she'll miss those stock options when the time comes to put together a down payment on her dream house. But no one knows anything for sure. No one ever has. That wedding may not be such a bad trade-off after all. In a time when great memories and the love of our friends and family are the only things we can reasonably hope to have any control over, we as employers have to be able to meet those expectations without losing our best talent and our best hopes for the future in the process.

CHAPTER 34

Soothing the Savage Skeptic

Skeptics aren't necessarily a bad thing to have around. In fact, as with the bacteria in yogurt, yeast, and your intestines, it's possible to have good skeptics in your corporate culture. They digest ideas, they promote growth, and they can help to cultivate an environment that doesn't support the really destructive element—the *cynic*. Skeptics, you see, withhold judgment until all the evidence is in. Cynics are actively hostile toward every new idea that comes along. Make friends with skeptics, get accustomed to an environment that encourages open debate, and you'll be giving yourself a chance to prove again and again that management really does mean what it says. Give the skeptics a reason to turn negative on you, and you'll have one heck of a cynical cadre on your staff. When skeptics finally come down on one side or the other—and you can be certain that they *will* make up their minds—make sure they come down on your side.

Wait a minute, you are thinking. "How could my company possibly have skeptics?" In your community and your industry, you're considered the best place to work. You're one of the nation's most admired

187

companies. You're family-friendly. You have rock-bottom turnover. And you've been in all the magazines—you know, the ones with the lists. How could you possibly have skeptics? Because you are the employer of adults. And adults have been around the block several times. And they read the newspapers. And they talk to their neighbors. And, when they were children sitting at the dinner table, they listened to their parents complain about *their* bosses. Because children of the 1980s and early 1990s saw their parents betrayed by their bosses and by their companies. Gone forever are the days when questioning one's boss at all was frequently seen as insubordination (especially in the military) and very often an actionable offense.

Even at Southwest we had our share of skeptics—even in our open-hearted, be-yourself-work-hard-and-thrive culture. Although as a company we might never have done anything to betray their faith in our word, we certainly had skeptics. New hires would come in not entirely believing everything they heard because they had been lied to before. I found that it would take them as much as three to four years of working at Southwest before they finally accepted the idea that the company stands by what it says.

The devastating economic hit that the airlines suffered after September 11, 2001, finally gave Southwest a chance to prove that it means what it says, in a very big way. Among the many different ways in which Southwest is notorious, it's notorious for two specific reasons. First, it doesn't lead the way in terms of setting pay scales, although the pay is within the market range, and when you add the stock options, profit sharing, and other benefits, the package is competitive. And it is especially competitive when the company does well. When the company does well, so do the employees. And second, Southwest has never laid off a single person because of economic hardship. During previous economic boom times, some of the other airlines would negotiate huge contracts with their labor unions, contracts that would inevitably result in losses during economic downtimes. And people at those airlines would get more cash than Southwest employees would. So pilots, mechanics, and ramp agents would start thinking, "I should be making as much as the employees doing the same work at other airlines."

We would have to respond by saying that we are in business to make a profit. Herb Kelleher frequently quoted Samuel Gompers, one of the fathers of the labor union movement, as saying that the greatest disservice that a company can do to employees is not to make a profit. At Southwest, making a profit was essential. Other airlines seemed to accept the idea that there would be periods during which they would lose money and have to lay people off. Southwest does not overhire and then lay people off during downturns. If you go through several turns of the economic cycle in the airline industry, the facts are plain. But the September 11 events proved once and for all that Southwest truly does walk its talk. The other airlines laid off hundreds of thousands of people after that devastating tragedy that continues to have ripple effects. Southwest didn't lay off one.

Southwest's actions were consistent to its word and past practices. And it was consistent over time, even when things got harder and harder. In their wisdom, Herb Kelleher, Jim Parker (the new CEO), and the team had known that the boom times couldn't last forever. Of course, no one could have foreseen how horribly they'd come to an end. Still, Southwest had the necessary foundation, built up over time by its consistent loyalty to its principles, a strong balance sheet, and good relationships with suppliers, to withstand the shock. And Southwest employees, new and long-time, got to see firsthand that their employer means what it says—even under the worst possible circumstances.

I pray that the world never again has a September 11 in which to demonstrate the authenticity of our policies toward our employees in such an extraordinary way. But that opportunity also comes day in and day out, under the most normal circumstances. This is when we can keep the skeptics engaged—even the most savage of skeptics, the ones about to go over to the dark side of cynicism.

This is how you keep skepticism healthy and on your side:

1. *Live the values you promote.* Mahatma Gandhi said, "Be the change you want to make." I would humbly like to add: Demonstrate your principles in the smallest of choices. You're being watched.

Closely. You make plenty of mistakes. Just be sure that none of your actions are inconsistent with your published principles, beliefs, and code of ethics.

2. *Be consistent over time.* Although one slip-up can destroy many years of carefully accumulated confidence, trust rarely develops in an instant or through an incident. Like the process of building a coral reef, huge results do happen, but they happen almost imperceptibly and over time. Have patience.

3. *When you make a mistake, instantly return to your published values and openly apologize from that platform.* Forget modifying phrases such as "it wouldn't have happened if," or "circumstances beyond our control," or "we had no idea what the other department was doing," or, the all-time favorite, "I don't recall." Own the mistake simply and comprehensively. And then spell out exactly how you intend to return to the correct course.

4. *Market the fact that you're staying the course.* Okay, so maybe your employees aren't earning the same pay as their peers in other similar companies. But they have one heck of a pay-for-performance plan. Or they're building incredible nest eggs for retirement. Or they own a larger piece of the company. Make sure your employees stay aware of that fact. Use internal publications, intranet communications, employee meetings, whatever is available to you to celebrate the fact that this is the best company your employees can choose to work for.

CHAPTER 35

The Most Important HR Policy: Throw Out the Policy Manual
(And Build Strong Managers Instead)

Just as much as it's known for the vast fortunes that have been made—and lost—there over the years, Silicon Valley is also known for its free-wheeling, fun-loving workplace style. And that makes a lot of sense. Innovation requires a sense of play; the same engineer who is designing a wireless telecommunications infrastructure for his employer may also be tinkering with an automated dog that fetches his newspaper and cruises the cubicles barking at startled coworkers. And, in the throes of the so-called war for talent, employers had to do anything and everything to captivate that inner child so that the outer genius could deliver the Next New Thing. That's why we had foosball tables, Sony Playstations, scooters, balls, and other toys on the job. For a while there, Silicon Valley was a veritable romper room.

So you can imagine my surprise when, during my first weeks at Yahoo!, I was greeted with, "Hi! Glad you're here! Would you please write a policy on this? Would you please write a policy on that?" Imagine their surprise when I said "No" and "No." I had barely set up my voice mail when I was flooded with requests for policies. Three of the better requests that I particularly remember were: no dogs allowed, no riding scooters in the hallways, and no bare feet in the cafeteria. All those requests seem reasonable. Why not make policies on these matters? Precisely because they *are* so reasonable. Any adult can see that scooters, bare feet, and dogs are usually inappropriate in the workplace. Why make a rule about it?

I developed a certain aversion to policies at Southwest, where you'd think that FAA regulations alone would have or could have put a stop to such hijinks as water-gun fights or beer and wine parties to celebrate milestones. When I first got to Southwest, there was a 350-page policy manual. We even had a policy that said that no one was allowed to order flowers. There were even policies about writing policies. These policies all had to be written a certain way, with a certain format, and officially approved. We all lived and breathed by that policy manual.

Until one day when Herb and my boss, Ann Rhoades, decided that the HR policies needed be to redone. Now that was a formidable idea. Where could we begin? With the flowers? But then Ann said one simple thing: "Why don't we just burn the policy manual?"

Well, we didn't actually put a match to the book, but we might as well have. We ruthlessly reduced it to about 35 pages of the most essential policies, those that were required by law or were key to our culture. So here was our new umbrella policy: If you can't find it in this new book, you're on your own. Make the decision yourself.

Managers were quite frightened by this development. But it was absolutely in keeping with our internal brand of freedom. We wanted a culture that gave employees a lot of leeway for having fun, making mistakes, and learning from those mistakes.

I think HR professionals as a breed are far too obsessed with rules. I once gave a speech to a SHRM chapter about the fun and merriment at Southwest. And I told the story of how one of my people department teammates had recently sent out an e-mail to everyone at the department saying that there would be a water-gun fight in the parking lot the next day (without my permission, I'm proud to add). I told the SHRM group how much fun everyone had had and how people were talking about it for months afterward. A few weeks later I received a message from a member of the audience saying this: "I would like to have a water-gun fight at my workplace. What are the rules?"

At a different event, I talked about the Southwest slogan that says, "We smile because we want to, not because we have to." Wouldn't you know it. SHRM's wonderful information center contacted me afterward passing on an inquiry about our *smile policy*! My answer: "We have these people who walk around with clipboards, and put a check mark by employees' names every time they're spotted smiling. For each time they're caught smiling they get an extra 25 cents in their paycheck." The person on the other end of the line was dutifully taking notes until I had to stop her: Just kidding!

At Yahoo!, the benefits manager was contacted by her counterpart at a nearby semiconductor manufacturer. The company had heard that we had foosball tables and wanted to know how we monitored their use. She jokingly explained that they are kept behind locked doors, and they're accessed by a card swipe. We can tell how much time the employee is at the tables and deduct that time from their paycheck. Again (in case you're tempted to quote this passage out of context), she was just kidding!

A few years ago, I was contacted by a consulting firm that was conducting a study on behalf of a very large company in the package delivery business. The company wanted to know if it could have a copy of our dress code policy for office workers at Southwest. I responded that we didn't have a dress code policy. Stunned, the person on the other line asked, "Is this really the head of HR?" When I replied in the affirmative, she asked, "Well, what do you do if someone comes to work dressed inappropriately?" I answered with my own question: "What would be inappropriate?" She responded, "Shorts and a T-shirt." I said, "That's what I am wearing right now!" We didn't need a policy, and if someone did push the envelope, we asked the person's manager to please discuss the problem with the person one on one. That usually fixed the problem.

At Southwest we trusted our people. We expected them to think independently, produce creative ideas, and pull together as a team. We realized that writing a rule for every significant situation had the potential to undermine the culture for which we had worked so hard. Our leaders were trained and encouraged to use their own good judgment and common sense as situations dictated.

Breaking the rules was often rewarded at Southwest in situations where people might have been reprimanded for it at other organizations. Rules and policies are sometimes necessary, but what's important is to do the right thing when tough situations arise. Employees who have a sense of ownership in the company will usually make the right decision for the company.

Shortly after being contacted by the consultant, I was contacted by the Director of Policy Development and Implementation (his title was really long, but this was the gist of it) for a large aircraft manufacturer located in the Pacific Northwest. He was charged with developing a new streamlined process for policy development at his organization, following a large merger. He asked, "What is your process for developing policy, vetting the policy, policy approval, and implementation?" I explained that our process was highly technical. I kept a file in my desk in which I put little notes, e-mails, memos, etc., of items that might need to become policy. These were suggested by other leaders, our legal department, or our experience in HR. About once a year, I revised the manual, adding new policies but always trying to subtract as much as I added. I discussed these ideas with my teammates in HR, and then with my boss, our COO, and the firm's general counsel. If they agreed, the new guidelines were official. The whole process took a couple of weeks, and we certainly didn't need a director and staff to make this happen.

If policies are so counterproductive, how can we keep some semblance of civilization on the job? What happens if someone is afraid of that real live drooly golden Lab who sits faithfully at the feet of its owner? What happens if a scooter runs amok and takes a chunk out of the drywall? Answer: Equip and empower your managers to deal with it.

If you see something going on that's dangerous, ask people to stop. If it's not dangerous, you should probably allow it.

When I talk about this with my HR buddies, I am often asked what we did when someone crossed the line of acceptability. I'm always reminded of a flight attendant who was trying to make her fellow crew members laugh aboard a flight that was only partially full. First she made faces, but that wasn't effective. Eventually, she mooned her coworkers from the back of the plane. She didn't think any customers would see her. But, unfortunately, one very conservative person turned around just as she was "dropping trou" and witnessed the momentary lapse of good judgment—among other things. The passenger wrote the company and complained. Herb wrote back and apologized, saying that "she had caught us with our pants down." And our vice president of flight attendants called this very embarrassed employee in for a discussion. She promised never to do it again, and, to the best of my knowledge, she remains one of the best flight attendants in the business to this day. Now, what kind of policy could possibly have anticipated and prevented that one?

"ITEM: Attention all employees: The removing of one's pants while on duty is grounds for immediate termination!"

I don't think so. In fact, I'd have to wonder about anyone who could anticipate this particular contingency.

Remember, everyone at work is an adult, even though some of them may not act that way at times. But that's when the fun usually begins.

Keep Policies Simple

■ Use common sense and simple language.

■ Minimize rules, meetings, forms, and levels of approval.

■ Keep communications open and straightforward.

■ Use the Golden Rule as your guide.

■ Learn by doing.

- Forgive and forget.

- Don't change the rules in the middle of the game.

- It doesn't have to be perfect, just good enough.

- Delegate and empower managers to manage their employees.

- Define how decisions are made.

- Be sure people know their span of control and their boundaries, and can operate within them.

- Trust people to do their jobs and think for themselves.

CHAPTER 36

Diversity Should Be From the Heart—Not Just By the Book

Sometimes the best intentions have accidental consequences. In our efforts to do the right thing, we create a monster that is awkward, ugly, and big. I have a serious objection to the diversity programs that we commonly see in the workplace. They actually promote discrimination. By placing the emphasis on people's differences (with some companies actually establishing a quota system), we end up resorting to a form of tokenism. We know we're doing it, but we're afraid to stop. We form diversity councils. We look at the numbers. We sponsor special functions celebrating affinity groups where we showcase *our* African-American participation, *our* Hispanic groups, *our* gay-lesbian groups, *our* women-in-nontraditional-roles groups. Group by group they stand up, are recognized, smile for the camera, and sit down again. But these groups also sit at separate tables in the company lunchroom. And there is no true blending and understanding among all the wonderful talent we have in the company.

We know we want a better way. There are no easy answers, but maybe we can change our approach to the challenge of making sure that our companies welcome all kinds of talent from all different sources. A diverse-from-the-heart company creates a culture that appeals to all the different communities. In this kind of company, the fact that someone is different from someone else doesn't affect that person's ability to move forward in the company and find success in his or her career. At a diverse-from-the-heart company, differences either are transparent or are used as bridges to create a more vibrant tapestry of talents, experiences, abilities, expertise, and frames of reference. They are *not* categories to be acknowledged at special dinners. A diverse-from-the-heart organization recognizes that an inclusive culture is attractive not only to employees, but also to customers.

But how do you make that happen without making a *thing* about it? How do you create true diversity without resorting to diversity programs? This shouldn't be an unnatural forced fit or tokenism or an HR-driven (or HR-imposed) program that no one really wants. True diversity should be everyone's responsibility. I have to admit that I have struggled with these issues throughout my career. Finally someone in the marketing department turned on the light bulb for me with one simple concept. He said, "It is not black or white, it is green." He pointed out that in order to increase our profits and market share, we had to market and advertise our services to diverse groups, based on pure demographics. That was the beginning of a significant internal change. Once we made a commitment to attracting and serving customers from diverse sources, the HR part of the equation became clearer. The CEO got it; senior management got it; everyone got it. It wasn't just the right thing to do, it was the best business decision we could make.

As the HR person, you may be the one responsible for compliance, being sure you're measuring everything that needs to be measured, reporting what needs to be reported, and recruiting among the communities you need to recruit among in order to reach out and create the mix you want. But sensitivity to inclusiveness should be systemic throughout the entire company. It should be a way of life, not another "annoying program imposed by HR."

Actually, it doesn't have to be imposed at all. Perhaps a better way of putting it is *evolved with deliberate purpose*. The two companies I've worked with most recently, Southwest and Yahoo!, are incredibly diverse. And they got there without any real effort and without top-down initiatives that were forced on the organization. Of course we had the usual policies to comply with the law, and we discussed the issues in leadership training. What worked best was to focus on hiring the best candidates, and those candidates happened to come from a wide variety of populations. And, along the way, we promoted a culture that says that we will treat one another with compassion and with respect. In both cultures, the companies encourage people to be themselves. And so people have to learn how to work with many, many people who aren't exactly like them.

But let's also face a fact of cultural life: As evolved as we truly believe ourselves to be, it is human nature for us to gravitate toward people who, on the surface at least, appear to be just like ourselves. Which is one explanation for why Sunday is the most segregated day of the week. Which also explains why the corporate lunchroom looks amazingly like a junior high school cafeteria. So we still have to work hard at creating a mix through our recruiting, training and development, and workplace culture programs.

Recruitment

Get the word out to all sections of society that you welcome one and all. One year at Southwest we created a full-page ad featuring a wide variety of employees (many different races, male and female, all ages). The caption read: "What do these employees have in common? Answer: They all love their job." Then we placed this advertisement in a diverse group of publications: our in-flight magazine, special-interest magazines, and local newspapers.

Advertise for employees where you advertise for customers. At Southwest we often advertised for customers on the *Tom Joyner Morning Show*, a nationally syndicated radio program for the African American audience. Tom actually had me on as a guest one morning. We had a ball, and when I gave out the URL for our recruiting web site, we got more hits on our web site that morning than we had ever had in a single day.

Training and Development

Provide leaders and employees with the knowledge and insight they will need if they are to foster diversity in the workplace and the marketplace. Make sure you have plenty of opportunities for everyone to move in and move up—someone's particular demographic isn't a barrier to success. In Silicon Valley, for instance, women in technical positions are experiencing barriers to promotions. Much of the reason is the high-pressure, start-up culture here (even among long-established firms), which dictates that employees dedicate long hours to their jobs. That may be perfectly fine for young, ambitious men with no families, but it doesn't help young, ambitious women who want a more balanced life that includes children. So, as employers in a high-tech culture, we must work very hard to create other career development paths for this very valuable segment of our workforce. And it's not only women who will benefit from this initiative. Anyone—woman or man—who wants a balanced life won't have to sacrifice his or her career and long-term success for the sake of family or other personal passions.

Training programs and other educational opportunities should eliminate barriers to entry for a wide variety of populations who might want to start their careers with your company. At Southwest we provided scholarships to members of the Organization of Black Airline Pilots so that more African American pilots could receive the necessary ratings to fly commercial jets. Southwest had the very first African American chief pilot in commercial aviation history. He was active in the pilot community and helped attract many minority pilots to our ranks. Southwest also gives scholarships to women pilots and has the highest percentage of women pilots of any airline.

The old-fashioned sensitivity training programs must still be in place. However, these programs should be for everyone, not just for the so-called average white male. Everyone needs to understand that people can be offended by certain comments or behaviors.

Unfortunately, this need for sensitivity training isn't going to go away anytime soon. I had hoped that as younger generations who had gone to school with a more diverse set of schoolmates came up after me, diversity and discrimination wouldn't be an issue anymore. But I've found that some of the younger employees still haven't learned what you can and what you can't say. They still have bad attitudes that have been passed down to them by their parents. I'm amazed to find myself saying to people still, "No, you cannot call someone a bad word that's disparaging to their race" or "No, you cannot promote someone who isn't the best candidate for the job simply because you like that person or that you want someone just like you in that position."

Diversity awareness must also encompass an understanding of the different needs of different *generations*. For about fifteen years now, we've been aware of the increasing numbers of people in what we call the "Sandwich Generation:" employees with both children and dependent parents. We've been learning a great deal about accommodating their needs and distractions without losing the valuable resource of their talents and abilities.

Now we're seeing another group coming up: young workers who have lived peripatetic lives. More and more members of younger generations grew up without the support systems that were in place in the past. They may not have lived in the same city for their entire lives; they may have moved frequently; they may not have had a strong family life. Perhaps their parents shared custody of them, and they moved from one parent's house to the other's every week. For better or worse, that kind of lifestyle has an impact on the way the children were formed into adults. All those family issues that we were dealing with in the 1980s and 1990s are now becoming workplace issues as the grown children enter the workforce.

New diversity issues will arise from having four generations in the workplace at one time. Having the new Generation Y group working side by side with Generation X, baby boomers, and seniors will call not only for sensitivity but also for creative HR programming. Benefits, compensation, and other offerings to employees must be designed to meet diverse needs.

A word about the diversity of diversity: Originally we thought of diversity as primarily addressing African American issues, then we quickly extended it to embrace Hispanic cultures. Very soon after that, we included an acknowledgment of all kinds of differences: gender, race, religion, sexual orientation, national background. I am now reading about diversity in size and appearance. And so diversity itself expands more and more to include new populations and demographics as they come up. Just when you think you might have this diversity thing down, it changes on you. That's all the more reason to make the *principles* of acceptance, respect, and equal treatment systemic in your organization, rather than focusing on the *process* of diversity programs.

CHAPTER 37

Use Your People Expertise to Create Successful Mergers and Acquisitions

No matter how the overall world economy is doing at any given time, it never stops crackling with the excitement of great ideas being developed behind the doors of hopeful start-ups. Economists and industrialists alike know that much of the future is not being developed in the glass-and-steel halls of megacorporations. It's being formulated in the garages, basement workrooms, sketchbooks, and low-rent loft spaces of dreamers throughout the world. Some of these little enterprises eventually become megacorporations. But most of the ones that survive and thrive are eventually courted, caught, and bought by large companies that don't want to grow their innovations from scratch. Why go through the expense and risk of research and development when the new product you need is for sale—complete and ready to roll out—at the little shop around the corner?

One possible answer is that if you don't take the necessary steps both before and after the acquisition, that little shop could very easily turn out to be the Little Shop of Horrors. Over the last ten years, the buying and selling frenzy has taken on a whole new energy. (Before the New Economy started showing us that there was some real money to be made, how many innovators do you think really thought in terms of an "exit strategy"? Ford? Edison? Pasteur? Curie? Hewlett? Packard? Even Jobs? I don't think so. Certainly not Gates.)

With every frenzy, there must come studies to measure it. The results are mixed, but the news is consistently worrisome. According to the findings, over half of all mergers and acquisitions fail—and some studies say that the failure rate may be as high as 80 percent. Much of the cause—culture clash, lack of communication and honesty, poor integration plans—can be laid directly at HR's doorstep. I'm not saying that HR is at fault for the past failures. But as the business climate continues to promote M&A as the way to acquire genius and innovation, this is a marvelous opportunity for HR to innovate new processes of its own and add real value to the companies—both the buyer and the seller. If you step in and get involved with the acquisition team from the very beginning, the difference you make to the process could mean jobs saved, jobs created, money made, and ultimately a very positive outcome all around. If you're not there or don't do your job well, none of the burning people issues are going to be addressed early on. They're going to pop up later, and it's going to be harder to fix them once the deal has been made and there's no turning back.

Where do you start getting involved? At the same point almost everyone else does.

The Due-Diligence Phase

Once the most senior leaders decide that they're going to go after a company, the experts begin to analyze the prospective purchase from the point of view of what they know best. The financial people will be evaluating what the financial situation will be. Can we make the numbers? Is the price right? Can we make money on this deal? The legal people will be making sure all the laws are followed. Are there big lurking legal problems we'll be taking on? Is there pending product liability litigation? The HR people should be looking for essential make-or-break issues as well: How does our objective for the acquisition match up with that of the company being acquired? Sit down with the leadership team and the CEO of the company that is being acquired and ask, "What are *your* goals for this?" Write down their answers. Then sit down with your corporate development people who are evaluating the potential acquisition and ask, "What are *your* goals?" You can see the big issues right away when you compare the two answers and look for disconnects.

In addition to comparing the expectations of the two companies, compare the cultures of the companies as well. Don't automatically assume that you're acquiring a spirited, maverick young pup full of independent drive. I've gone into very small companies that we were about to acquire, only to discover they have a completely autocratic style. If the leader of the organization has been autocratic, he or she is probably surrounded by people who can't make decisions on their own. So if the leader leaves the company after the deal, the whole next team directly under the leader will probably go too. And you're still going to have big people issues. I once evaluated, in the "due-dilly" stage, a smaller company that had an unbelievable amount of process and discipline. My organization didn't have nearly so much. Ultimately, this resulted in a decision not to do the deal. Make a point of sitting down with your HR counterpart and auditing the company's HR program.

During the due-diligence phase, you're looking for two things. First, is there any reason why we shouldn't buy this company? Is there going to be an unforeseen financial situation? There are often very expensive, unforeseen financial situations involving HR that finance folks or the lawyers might not think to look for. Are the 401(k) or pension plans properly administered? If not, you may be taking on the liability for fines or the disqualification of the whole plan, which becomes an expensive burden. Are there any benefit plans that are not in compliance with the law? Are there outstanding claims or lawsuits or charges of discrimination from employees? Is there a sexual harassment case looming? Are there any expensive union issues on the horizon?

The second determination you want to make is, what kind of talent does the company have? Whom do you really want to keep? Who is the most valuable to your company's objectives, and who is the least valuable? Work with your HR counterpart in the other company to create powerful retention and severance programs, both of which broadcast the lasting message that people are important to your company.

Bear in mind that you may be working in partnership with someone whose days are also numbered. Most HR people are realistic and know the score. They're well aware that they may not stay after the deal closes. But they still want to help make the acquisition successful and are happy to work on it.

This is also the time to pick up on the "vibes" of the organization—the intangibles that will tell you in subtle or not-so-subtle ways that you have a deal. Are the people representing the company to be acquired open with you, or do you have this nagging feeling that they're hiding something? Gut feelings are real. Think about what led you to feel that way and ask others on your team if they are getting the same feeling.

In the due-diligence phase, your job isn't *just* to collect information. It's also to report it back honestly to the M&A team that's making the ultimate decision. If you've got discouraging news to share on the matter, this isn't going to win you many popularity points. But you have to do it anyway. During this phase, when people are buying something they're in love with, they don't want to hear anything bad about their object of desire—or, shall we say, object of *acquire*. But if you've got inside information, insight, or even an intuitional inkling that something might be a showstopper, they need to hear about it.

If your team is determined to go ahead with the acquisition despite all the evidence that it might be a bad idea (or that it at least deserves deeper investigation), you're going to have to draw on and stand on every last ounce of the credibility and confidence that you've cultivated during your time at the company. That's hard to do when you're relatively new yourself. But if you stand up for what you believe in and are proved right, your credibility will grow in very short order. If you have strong negative feelings about the leadership team of a company that your company is acquiring, express those feelings. You might advise that keeping the CEO may not be the best alternative.

If you discover that your company's objectives for the merger are totally different from those of the company to be acquired, you will have to determine whether the upside in revenue and profit is worth the pain of having to replace many of the top team members. If culture is the issue, can you change the way things are done through communication, training, leadership, and mentoring? Or is the difference too great to overcome?

The Integration Phase

Once the deal is made, the way HR participates in the integration process could be the single most important factor in improving the odds that the new relationship will be a success. Most companies are going to put together a detailed integration process, and HR had better take a central part in it. In fact, integration *is* HR. You must be ready to answer these questions:

- Who are you going to keep?

- What kind of severance package are you going to offer the others?

- What kind of retention program are you going to install to make sure that your most valued performers remain?

- How are you going to evolve your compensation and rewards program to blend the two organizations?

- Can you cross-pollinate the two newly merged cultures to begin the blending process? Whom from inside headquarters can you assign to the new acquisition, and whom from the new acquisition can you bring into headquarters for a developmental assignment?

■ How will you handle benefits programs?

■ When will you roll over the payroll?

Communication is, of course, the essential ingredient for success. You have to communicate 100 times more than you think you do. Every moment that you don't spend telling employees what you're doing and what they can expect from you is a moment when they'll be filling the news holes with their own hypotheses, gossip, and assumptions. There are two outcomes you can count on: (1) They'll be wrong, and (2) the conclusions they draw will probably be the worst-case scenarios and will damage morale, trust, and strength inside your company. The very people you want to keep are the people whom you'll lose fastest. They're the best, so they can walk out and get another job if they have to. The people who are the worst are hanging on by their fingernails. So you really need to communicate to the best: "We want to keep you." Don't just assume that they can wait a month before they know their future. Most people, if they're really sharp, will be polishing up their résumés just in case or may have already begun the interview process when they first suspected that the company might be sold. So you will benefit from being as forthcoming with as much of the truth as you can as early you can and as often as you can. There cannot be too much communication.

There is a tremendous amount of pain and fear and stress associated with every merger and acquisition. People fear that they're going to lose their jobs. Or they fear that they won't like their jobs under a new parent company or with a new manager. Or they fear that they might have to uproot their families and move across the country in order to keep their jobs. They fear losing coworkers that they love working with. They worry about being yanked off of projects they've poured their heart, soul, and many long hours into, only to be placed in some dreary Big Corporation bureaucratic bayou. There's plenty to worry about. And your people will be looking for some definitive answers. If they don't get them when they need them, they'll make them up on their own.

Communicate!

CHAPTER 38

"In the Unlikely Event of an Emergency"

Every industry and every profession has its own set of acronyms. We reduce to three or four letters those topics that (1) are a mouthful to actually say again and again, (2) are tongue twisters, (3) are frequently discussed, or (4) are too dreadful and hideous to be fully considered but nonetheless have to be discussed. In the world of aviation, for instance, HR stands for something completely different. In aviation, HR stands for "human remains," and that means cargo rather than talent.

And however hideous and dreadful it might be, the possibility that our customers and employees might perish in a horrible crash was a contingency that we at Southwest had to consider and anticipate. Up until September 11, 2001, most companies consciously or subconsciously put themselves on a sliding scale of disaster potential. There would have been no argument anywhere, for instance, that an airline would be more prone to a large-scale disaster than, say, a bond trading firm—whose employees, up until September 11, would have been most at risk for maybe carpal tunnel syndrome, a heart attack, or a paper cut. In fact, according to one of the profiles in *The New York Times'* "Portraits of Grief," one of the people who died in the World Trade Center had recently quit her job as a flight attendant because she was sure that a desk job downtown would be safer.

As employers, one of the lessons we must learn from of September 11 is that disaster can strike no matter who we are, where we are, or what kind of industry we're involved in. It could be a product-related disaster, like the infamous Tylenol sabotage incident, or it could be a disaster that involves our employees, like September 11, or the Oklahoma City bombing, or a disgruntled employee taking it out on his coworkers with an automatic weapon, or an international kidnapping. How we prepare for such dreadful eventualities—and how we cope with them if they do occur—is an extraordinary opportunity for HR to take the lead and reinforce in the hearts and minds of our constituencies the idea that we really are committed to being employers who care deeply about our customers, our employees, and our community.

Unfortunately, unless you're in a high-risk business like aviation, it's easy to be so distracted by day-to-day business issues that you put off laying down a contingency plan for when the unthinkable happens. If *you* take the initiative to create this plan, you can guarantee that the corporate response will be based on caring, authenticity, employee well-being, and communication. So maybe you should use the fact that you're reading this chapter as a sign to stop putting it off.

Dealing With the Unthinkable

■ *Assemble an Emergency-Response Task Force.* The key players should include the heads of security, public relations, operations, and facilities; a union official, if you're unionized; and someone from government affairs (especially if you're closely regulated by the local, state, or federal government). If you're a significant employer in your region, you might consider exploring ways of including law enforcement in the group—at least as guest participants in your meetings now and then.

■ *Design a Master Plan for Handling Disasters.* If you might need to set up an emergency command center, where would it be located?

Identify an alternative location off-site in case your on-site center is destroyed in the disaster. (The New York City and Port Authority command centers, as well as important FBI offices, were destroyed in the World Trade Center; much of the disaster management was conducted in a nearby public elementary school, with adults sitting on kindergarten chairs planning the next steps of a scenario that they had never imagined in their wildest nightmares.) Assign protocols for every general type of emergency or disaster. Make sure those protocols are consistent with your company's overall philosophy about communication and relationships. At what point, for instance, does public relations begin contacting the media? (Or, more realistically, when does PR start answering the calls that are already flooding its office?) When is a total lockdown of the property appropriate, and when is it not? What role should the CEO have in leading the company back toward more stability? What kinds of phone numbers should be established? Should they be disseminated to employees and the outside community now, before anything has happened? What data should be immediately secured and made unavailable for public consumption? (In the airline industry, for instance, any time a plane goes down, the airline will pull all reservation data out of the computers to prevent the media from publishing names before the airline has had the chance to contact relatives.) How will you maintain normal operations to meet customer needs?

■ *Plan to communicate with your employees more frequently and comprehensively than with the general public.* Frequent and thorough employee communication must be an essential element of the response plan. If the public relations office issues three releases to the public, make sure your employees get five updates. Emails and closed-circuit videos streamed directly to their monitors are two ways you can keep employees current on unfolding events minute by minute, if that's possible. Taped phone announcements are another great way of keeping news flowing so that no one is forced to surmise, guess, or crank up the rumor mill.

■ *Be prepared to lead the leader.* As leadership lessons began to emerge from the events of September 11, there was a lot of discussion about the importance of the leaders being visible to the employees right away. The next time confusion and anxiety strike your workplace, that lesson might be quickly forgotten as your CEO concentrates all of his or her attention on the business of running—or saving—the business. Your job will be to make sure the CEO stays connected with the people. The CEO might honestly think that there's nothing new to say, or that his or her time is best spent coping with the emergency. A simple walk through the building, a sandwich in the cafeteria, every effort that the CEO takes to be visible, to be calm, to be informed, and to be informative will be remembered and valued for decades to come when employees recall a day that changed their lives forever.

When in the Course of Human Events . . .

A business plan may be what creates a business. But a community of people is what creates a company. And for every person who works in your company, you have an epic saga unfolding: births, marriages, illnesses, celebrations, and deaths. Hundreds of personal milestones are celebrated inside companies every year—perhaps even every day. But it's on those days when an employee loses a loved one that a strong showing of company support and unity means the most. When my father died, there were many Southwest people at the funeral, people he never knew, but people who knew me and cared enough to stand by me in one of my most intensely personal and devastating moments. Herb and Colleen were both there, which was very meaningful, but what I'll cherish most is the collective message of love and support from a group that I worked with every day.

In the same spirit, when one of the company's own leaders dies, it means a lot to the family to see a showing of the employees. We have at least three different families in our lives: the one we're born into, our family of friends, and our family of coworkers. Considering the many, many hours that leaders spend away from their own families and devote to their work, it comes as a great comfort to grieving family members to see such a demonstration of respect and affection from the employees. (At Southwest we would attend funerals in full uniform.

212

The message of enduring love that this transmitted was unmistakable.)

Whether the emergency is a personal one, a corporate one, or a national devastation, the ability of the employees to pull together and stand by one another may make the difference between a company that heals and one that is crippled by the tragedy. No one else will be focused on the community of hearts and hands that can join in support of recovery. It will be up to you to make it happen. It could be your shining hour.

CHAPTER 39

Judgment Day Made Simple and Painless

Much to the chagrin of HR leaders around the globe, there is an annual event in the life of almost every working adult that may be dreaded even more than tax time: performance evaluation season. Those who aren't in HR or in a supervisory role are lucky. They only have to dread it once—that moment of truth when *their* turn comes for the feedback discussion meeting. But, sadly, those in management or supervisory positions—those who actually have to conduct the reviews—must relive those terrible moments over and over with each nervous employee who is sitting on the other side of their desk waiting for the year's judgment.

As a rule, no one really relishes the typical annual performance review. Who likes to be judged? And who really likes to be the one sitting in judgment? No one likes to judge other people's performance (who, after all, is perfect?). The potential for emotional confrontation is unbearable. A huge, ugly scene might ensue. Besides that, the forms are cumbersome, the process is time-consuming, and it takes managers away from what they perceive to be more important work. And if you're the manager, you have someone's livelihood—the security of entire families—in the palm of your hand. Who wants to be responsible for that?

The art and science of performance management is probably the most analyzed, studied, and written about (and hated and dreaded and controversial) of all HR-driven activities. While there is general agreement that performance management and performance improvement are core practices of best-run organizations, when the *moment of truth* actually comes around, the whole emotional culture surrounding the performance review meeting takes on a feel that's not too distant from that of a medieval torture chamber. Is it any wonder that the performance review meeting is one of the most commonly postponed meetings on any supervisor's calendar? But when these meetings are postponed, great performers go unrecognized and unrewarded, poor performers aren't given the chance to improve that they deserve, and jerks are allowed to continue to pull down the entire team.

There is a simple and effective way to bring performance management out of the Dark Ages and turn it into a positive process that supports a high-performance culture all year round.

The Best Annual Performance Review is the Daily Performance Review

Nobody likes to be told that he or she is not meeting expectations. But what's even worse is being told that you haven't been meeting expectations *for some time,* and that no one has told you this and consequently you have not been able to make the necessary improvements. Frequent, on-the-spot feedback—both good and bad feedback—not only keeps performance and productivity high, but also fosters trust, confidence, and the ability to actually focus on the work at hand, rather than worrying about where you stand.

As HR partners, we know that the quality of employees' performance and their capability is the core responsibility of any people leader all year long. Since it's a year-round issue for us, it should be a year-round issue for our employees. So why save up our concerns and recognition for one high-intensity hour out of the year? This is where we get ourselves into stressful trouble. We observe poor performance and think to ourselves, "Here's something to mention during the review," but we don't fix the problem right then and there.

The next step is to link individual goals to business and departmental objectives. A culture that supports ongoing, daily performance feedback depends on group fluency with the organization's business plan and the goals and objectives that support that plan. Each department, function, or business unit must have its deliverables to help the organization meet those goals. And then each individual has his or her job description, competencies, accountabilities, and behaviors that support the department's and the company's objectives. Individual goals and objectives are set by employees and their immediate supervisors to ensure that employees are focused on the right things. This becomes an annual performance plan and will eventually become the basis for the yearly performance meeting.

The performance plan for each individual is a living, breathing document. It doesn't sit in a file until the end of the review period. Each quarter, leaders meet with their employees to make sure that the employees are on target and on schedule for meeting their goals. If someone is behind, this is the leader's chance to address the issues before the department as a whole gets too far behind. This is also the chance to discover whether the staff is getting the resources it needs to achieve its goals (the leader's performance is also under review here).

Both the annual and the quarterly meetings, however, are supported by the most important process of all: daily feedback and regular review meetings. When you see people do something really well, tell them so. Then make a note of it. And when you see a need for improvement, tell them that as well, as soon as you notice it. And make a note of that, too. My favorite method of keeping track is supremely low-tech. I make notes on simple pieces of paper and tuck them into a folder in my desk to keep them current and collected. But you can use any tracking method that works for you, as long as it's secure, so that you protect your employees' privacy and dignity.

Those little notes that you take on an ongoing—daily—basis will be your valuable record of corrections, improvements, and celebrations when the time comes for a focused face-to-face review meeting (notice that I didn't say *annual*). And remember, the rule is that you cannot write it down unless you have discussed it. Then you will know that the details that are discussed at review meetings will never be a surprise.

The Best Performance Review Tool Is a Blank Sheet of Paper

HR experts have spent decades trying to develop the scientifically perfect performance review tool, one that is guaranteed to be effective at improving performance and/or proving fairness should a legal situation arise. As far as I'm concerned, we've been spending a lot of time and money on a useless mission. My favorite tool is a blank sheet of paper—used regularly and often.

Now that we've established the need for frequent (not just annual) reviews, here's what you do with that piece of paper: Make notes on the answers to three questions for each employee:

1. How are you doing and what do you need to improve?

2. Where are you going?

3. As your boss, what do I need to do and know to help you do your job better?

Since, ideally, you and your employees have been keeping current with each other on their daily performance, nothing that comes out of this meeting should be a shock to either you or your employee. It should really serve as mainly a recap, perhaps a small renegotiation of your mutual expectations or reengineering of the processes—whatever it takes to keep and grow great employees who are performing up to their potential.

Those notes will serve as the formal record of your employee's responsiveness to both suggestions for improvement and praise for good performance. They reflect a culture of frequent communication and thorough documentation that is both effective for the company and considerate of the employee's need to understand what is required in order to do well.

There Are No Bad Surprises

Engaging leaders and employees in this culture of ongoing feedback takes the worry out of the performance management process. No one can say that she's been blindsided when she has been consistently told what she does that's great and where she needs improvement.

And leaders and their organizations are protected in those rare situations when an employee is in total denial of all the negative feedback that he has received before. Train your leaders to ask employees, "How do you think you're doing?" Over 90 percent will deliver an accurate self-report based on your previous conversations and the actions they've taken (or haven't taken) to remedy problems. But a few will say, "What do you mean my performance is below expectations? I've done great work here!" And then the leader will be able to reach into a full file of notes and say, "Let's take a look. Here are notes on all the discussions we've had. Does this look like good performance?"

Train leaders to use a calm questioning style, inviting employees to draw their own conclusions based on the past record—not the record of their performance, but the record of frequent discussion of their performance.

If employees receive frequent feedback designed to help them improve their performance, they will know as well as the leaders do what their best next step might be. In fact, they may be one step ahead of you!

CHAPTER 40

Parting Company

I can't think of a single person who entered the HR profession because he or she loves firing people. Whether terminations are voluntary or involuntary, the separation process is among the least-preferred duties that well-meaning HR leaders face. The termination represents a disappointment, a failure that appears to be beyond repair. It's devastating for everyone concerned.

But it can be made less devastating. In fact, if you consider the termination process as just another phase in the entire lifespan of the relationship between your company and your employee, it can actually be an opportunity to save the relationship over the long term. Ultimately, if you truly regard your company as a customer service enterprise first, this is your chance to deliver extraordinary service to a customer who needs you now more than ever. When you're parting company—no matter what the circumstances may be—you can do it in such a way that the employee feels just as good going out the door as he or she did coming into the company.

There *are* positive outcomes that can be had from the termination experience: deeper self-knowledge for both the manager and the departing employee, the opportunity for the employee to learn from mistakes and avoid repeating them in the future, a chance for the manager to learn how to improve his own performance management practices, the opportunity for the company as a whole to build a new kind of relationship with its employees, and even the chance to reclaim that employee as a newly rededicated worker with a promising future with your company.

The termination process may not necessarily be the end of the line with your employee. But, whether the employee stays or goes, it can be your last chance to make the story a happy one.

Involuntary Separation

Let's start with the hardest one first. Involuntary separations present the most potential for pain.

The good news is that if your company's managers stay on top of their performance management, truly agonizing involuntary separations will be a rarity. Except for the most egregious infractions, involuntary terminations are hardly ever spontaneous. The termination should never be a surprise. Anyone who is fired should have seen it coming a long time ago—and should have been *given the chance* to see it coming a long time ago. The manager should have made it clear well in advance of this moment that the ultimate consequence of the objectionable performance level or behavior would be firing. Too many managers are so uncomfortable with these make-or-break warnings that they tiptoe around the point for fear of hurting their employee's feelings. So how clear is clear? Let me spell it out for you. Use these words:

"If this behavior (or performance problem) does not stop, you will be fired." Period.

With the consistent feedback that accompanies the culture of ongoing performance management, poorly performing employees are just as dissatisfied as their manager is. And so the reward of ongoing performance management is not just the best possible chance of having an improving employee, but also the best possible chance of having a nonimproving employee resign well before you're ready to terminate that person. Voluntary separations are rarely welcome, but in these cases they come as a blessed relief. So, if no other argument for ongoing performance management has yet convinced you, perhaps this one will: People who are constantly criticized and corrected hate their job as much as you don't like having them there. And they will be more likely to eject themselves before you have to push that button.

The involuntary separation process is your last chance to make sure that the employee is absolutely beyond redemption. And, without countermanding the manager's decision, you still have a chance to reclaim worthy employees who are in fact dedicated workers and may deserve one more chance. I've had several opportunities to reclaim employees who really did merit another try. One man, for instance, was fired for excessive lateness and absences. After repeated and fair warnings, he was again late one morning, and he was terminated as promised. While I didn't routinely investigate every single termination, I did look into this one, because the story he told me when he requested a review of his termination was compelling. As it turned out, a tragicomic series of events explained his tardiness: He had lost all his worldly possessions in a California earthquake and was sleeping on a mattress on the floor, with his alarm clock carefully placed by his head. During the night his two-year-old had toddled into it, knocking it over and turning it off. How can you not give that person one more chance?

In a separate instance, we came very close to losing a fabulous customer service representative in a hard-to-hire location. She was delightful, she was well educated, and she loved the company. We were thrilled to have her. However, a few weeks after she was hired, she discovered that she was pregnant, and she didn't want to be. Her choice was to have an abortion, but she suffered emotionally after the fact. This caused her to miss too much work during her probationary period. Her supervisor could tell that she was a fabulous worker—when she was there. But, as a unionized employer, we had work rules that were not flexible, and she had exceeded the maximum number of allowable absences. We had no choice but to let her go. She was too embarrassed to share her complete story with her boss, but in a last-ditch effort to keep her job, she told me the whole saga. And so I investigated it. I called her manager to find out what kind of employee she had been. Wonderful! The best in customer service! That's a hard employee to let slip through our fingers. Still, I had to support our attendance standards. So I let her termination stand, *but* I also invited her to reapply in six months. She rejoined Southwest after the six-month period passed, and to the best of my knowledge she's been working there ever since as one of the best in customer service. In this case we were able to use the termination process to actually retain a good employee in the long run, all the while supporting our managers and upholding our performance expectations.

Voluntary Separation

Even in times of high unemployment, companies need to go the extra mile to hang on to their best employees. By the time good performers decide on their own that it's time to seek out new opportunities, they have already decided that their current job is the limit of their future potential with the company. And they may be very wrong. For this reason, employers need to thoroughly investigate the reasons why people are leaving, and whether there is anything they can do to persuade them to stay. The exit interview, therefore, is more than just a pro forma, clipboard question-and-answer period. It's one of the company's best opportunities to save hundreds of thousands of dollars in turnover costs.

Always ask your departing employees, "Is there anything we could have done to keep you here?" You may be amazed at the answers. By the time the departing employee reaches your office, she has probably already concluded that there is no hope for accommodation with her boss. I've reclaimed great employees who simply needed more flexible hours to take care of family needs. For some reason, their bosses took a rigid stance about flextime, and I was able to step in and work things out before we lost great employees for good.

Or perhaps employees don't realize what a wide variety of opportunities there are within the company. When a valued employee has to relocate to another part of the country for private reasons, as far as the boss knows, that person has simply quit. End of story. But during the exit interview, your interviewer may discover that the employee loves his job, loves the company, and is heartbroken at the prospect of having to leave. If the employee doesn't already have another job lined up, maybe you can work things out: Perhaps you can set up a telecommuting arrangement. Or you can set up a part-time or work-sharing arrangement that keeps this high performer in your system, even if it's on a more limited basis.

The Inevitable End of the Line

Whether the departure is voluntary or involuntary, most people leave their employers at least a couple of times in their lives. This means that as HR leaders we're recycling and sending back out into the marketplace millions of employees every year. Those that we lose are brought on board by our colleagues. And those that they lose are the ones we recruit. Wouldn't it be nice to know that our new hires are not only experienced but also *wiser* for that experience?

Before you wind up your exit interview with the departing employee, take a few extra moments to ask the question: If you had the last three months to live over again, what do you think you would do differently? What have you learned that you can take with you to your next job? What are you proud of from your time here? What goals did you meet? What accomplishments will you be able to take with you?

When you see the termination process as an opportunity to connect with your employees on this deeper, more human level, you'll learn more about the culture of your company (and whether the reality matches expectations), and you'll learn more about yourself. And your departing employee not only will be equipped to be even more successful in the next job but will also leave your company smiling.

Smiling and satisfied. Isn't that the name of the game for a customer service organization?

CHAPTER 41

The Time to Plan for Layoffs Is *Before* You Do the Hiring

The way Southwest Airlines is run gives its employees and its leadership plenty to be proud of. But in the immediate aftermath of September 11, when the airline industry was hit especially hard, Southwest was distinguished by two extraordinary facts: (1) Thus far, it has stayed in the black while other airlines were running huge deficits, and (2) while those same airlines were sloughing off thousands upon thousands of employees, not a single person was laid off at Southwest. How could that be? It was largely the result of a fundamental principle that drives Southwest's management and HR decisions no matter what is happening in the marketplace: Manage in the good times as if times were bad.

Even though, as HR professionals, we all complain about layoffs and are horrified by the binge/purge nature of the employment cycle, we have come to accept the layoff process as a painful fact of life that revisits us with every twist of the cycle. While I certainly don't want to oversimplify the very complicated issues that are associated with layoffs, I would like to offer this one idea: HR is part of the problem.

The Time to Plan for Layoffs Is *Before* You Do the Hiring

Actually, I'd venture to say that more often than not, our senior leaders and we *are* the problem. In boom times, we get swept up in a voracious fit of recruitment, sucking up new employees like there's no tomorrow. Convincing ourselves that there's a talent shortage and panicking at the idea that our competitors will get the good people first, we grab and gobble up anyone and everyone with any semblance of ability who walks into our company. We all know that we are over-hiring, but the sense of urgency translates into the idea, "If we don't hire them, someone else will, so we'd better grab them fast!" Hiring is often the easy answer, rather than considering the alternatives. When we're making money and the feeling is "go! go! go!" it's easy—although irresponsible—to take on extra people. But the instant cash flow begins to tighten up, the people—that talent we so eagerly recruited and built space for—are among the first places we cut. And in case you're thinking that you might be the one handing *out* the pink slips, HR is one of those departments that routinely gets gutted in bad times. (In my very first job in HR, I was assigned to prepare the layoff packages for my company, which was terrible. Afterward, when I confided to my boss that it had been a particularly difficult day, he said, "It's about to get even tougher. You have one more layoff package to prepare for yourself." That was some welcome to the HR profession.)

The best layoff plan is the plan to avoid layoffs altogether. The time to implement such a plan is before you go into a massive hiring phase. First, the talent plan must be linked to the business plan. Any additions to staff should be cost-justified and shown to drive incremental business results. Work with your executive team to ensure that responsible decisions about staffing levels are made. Many executives are so accustomed to the up-and-down cycles that they fail to consider the alternatives. And our job is to present various options for consideration. Sit around a table with the HR team and ask yourselves, "When the economic cycle falls apart again, what are we going to do? How do we want to be regarded in our community, in our profession, in our industry? Let's think about what steps we're going to take now to prevent pain later." Once the HR team has a strategy to recommend, have the same conversation with the senior leaders of the company. There may still be a layoff in the future, but if you develop a plan based on these questions in advance, it may be a little less painful. In fact, it might even engender a little more trust, not diminish it.

By thinking outside the proverbial box before growing the company, you may be in a better position to acquire talent creatively without committing to long-term relationships that you can't sustain.

One approach to growing as needed is to pursue the contingent workforce solution, such as temporary workers and/or independent contractors. Identify positions that you might not need next year, and fill them on a contractual basis that retains employees for a short period of time—say a one-year renewable contract. (Make sure you follow IRS rules and have policies that define these work relationships to protect both the workers and the company.) Pay these people more in exchange for the mutual understanding that when the time comes to lay people off, they will be the first to go.

Identify which jobs might go away in bad times and which jobs aren't high-potential long-term key contributors. Which of those positions could you outsource?

Use flexible workers who are willing to work part-time, work on flexible schedules, or telecommute. Stay-at-home parents and retirees often enjoy working for a period of time and then taking longer periods of time off. According to the "SHRM Workplace Forecast: A Strategic Outlook 2002–2003," a research initiative conducted with the AARP and Roper Worldwide, Inc., 80 percent of the baby boomers plan to work at least part-time during their retirement years. This will be a significant source of talent in the future, and organizations that are able to meet the needs of this group will benefit from having very capable talent. Offer customized compensation and benefits programs for these workers, and explain that they may not be needed if business conditions change.

Find innovative ways to retool and retrain your existing workers. A few years ago, when IT talent became so scarce that we couldn't fill our needs, Southwest developed a Systems Boot Camp. Employees with some background in IT (schooling or a little experience) who met certain criteria were placed in a nine-week full-time training course in computer programming. Ramp agents, clerks, administrative assistants, financial associates, and others were trained and soon were working in IT. Some of these employees were able to double their salaries in a year. Almost all participants successfully completed the program. Very few companies lay off massive numbers of employees across the board. Most companies, even those that are downsizing a function or two, are struggling to hire in different areas or business units. So rather than laying people off, can you train them to fill those hard-to-fill jobs? If you can, you will have some intensely loyal talent.

Use technology in the best possible ways. Can you avoid throwing people at the problem by installing technology to do the work of people?

Provide life training, as well as job and skills training, to prepare people for whatever may happen. Empower people to plan their own careers and to consider what they might do in the future if what they are doing right now doesn't work out in the long term. This concept is healthy for workers and the company alike.

Before you lay off your first employee, consider other cost-cutting initiatives. There is so much waste in corporate America. Millions can be saved by reducing travel expenses, reducing spending on office equipment and supplies, discount purchasing, reducing overtime and premium pay, reducing vacation liability, cutting the costs of health care or workers' compensation, renegotiating vendor relationships, eliminating consultants, and delaying capital expenditures. At Recognition International, we had an expression, "Spend Recognition dollars as if they were your own." Every employee was encouraged to ask, "If this were my money, would I spend it this way?" At Southwest, low costs are a way of life. When everyone understands the important link between low costs and low fares in the business model, saving money can actually be a fun, team-building experience.

If you have to lay off employees, get input from your people. Can you include voluntary reductions, sabbaticals, or early retirements in the mix or find other ways to minimize the human loss? Can you offer unpaid time off? Will an across-the-board reduction in pay or benefits solve the problem? Be really innovative. Can you lend your people to another employer who might need them for a year-long assignment? Can you let them go to nonprofits for a year at a reduced salary while retaining their seniority and benefits? If you have to reduce your staff temporarily, but you want to make sure that these people are within your reach once you're ready to ramp up again, ask those who can afford it to take a sabbatical. But make it a sabbatical with lasting value: Offer to give them a meaningful bonus if they used the time to either go back to school, teach at a school, or work for a charity.

When it comes to the actual reduction in force, plan the process carefully. Keep employees' feelings at heart. I have heard so many stories of employees who suffered a secondary assault because they were not allowed to leave with dignity. Yesterday these people were trusted coworkers. Trust them as much as you can on their way out. While security concerns and risk avoidance are, of course, important in these situations, don't treat people whose jobs are being eliminated like criminals. Provide them with a bridge to their next opportunity. Employ outplacement firms or take other initiatives to help them go on to their next opportunities. Sponsor job fairs for your employees, and give companies that are hiring an opportunity to recruit the people who are departing.

Know which people and which functions you want to hang on to. Employers have become expert in cutting deep and ruthlessly. Unfortunately, it's become an accepted fact of layoff life that you are more at risk of losing high-performing talent (those who are confident they can find new and better opportunities somewhere else) than you are of stripping away the less-desirable performers. It's just as important—if not more important—to know which employees you aggressively want to keep as it is to know which employees you want to lose and which positions you want to shut down. Make your decisions and actions consistent with those priorities. The consistency you demonstrate will engender trust and respect among all employees—including the ones you may eventually lay off.

Everyone—including you—will then be able to say honestly that you saw it coming.

CHAPTER 42

... And Then Someone Said, "No Good Deed Goes Unpunished"

HR work often involves serving others. We can really serve only when we are deeply connected to the purpose. The very concept of being in service often implies that one is willing to be used by others now and then. How do we serve, and lead, without feeling abused?

My aspiration as a leader in HR is to model the principles of *servant leadership*. In his book, *Servant Leadership*, Robert Greenleaf described the fusion of servant and leader in one role—servant leadership. This style of leadership begins with a leader's natural inclination to serve, and that choice drives the person to lead in order to serve the needs of others successfully and meaningfully. Greenleaf's measure of servant leadership was whether or not those who were served became healthier, wiser, freer, more autonomous, and more likely to become servant leaders themselves.

Even with these lofty visions, I have to admit that there have been moments, days, and even weeks when I have felt more used or violated than lifted up by the intrinsic rewards that come from serving. I ask myself: "Why am I doing such a thankless job?" In the very act of serving and leading, in trying to help someone, my efforts don't work the way I intended them to. I try to help someone save her job when she should have been fired, and she sues the company for discrimination and names me as the perpetrator. I spend hours with a team member helping him to overcome an obstacle to his career advancement, only to find out that he has spread the word among his inner circle that I am too tough on him and push too hard. I explain in detail to a coworker why she wasn't given an expected promotion, and she comes to the bizarre conclusion that I "just don't like her." I plan and execute an incredible awards event, only to have one highly placed person complain because the line at the bar was too long.

HR is fraught with pressures and last-minute situations that make it difficult to enjoy every minute. The frenetic pace, the irate employee, the hiring manager who doesn't like any of the twelve qualified candidates he has interviewed, the person who feels underpaid and unappreciated are daily occurrences that can lead you to feel that the many things that you do well go unnoticed.

When I have these days, I try to keep a smile on my face and remind myself and others of the great work that we do and the difference we make. Former SHRM CEO and President Mike Losey put it best as he retired from a forty-year career in HR: "Unlike accountants who work with numbers, or engineers who work with tools and materials, we in HR work with people. That responsibility alone provides us with an opportunity to touch their lives, in many more ways than we will ever know. I believe that if we do our jobs well, we'll have the satisfaction of knowing that we have affected others in positive ways. But if we don't do it well, rarely are we given the opportunity to go back and correct our mistakes. That's our challenge, and for many of us, that's our calling. My hope for the HR profession is that it becomes our legacy" (*HR Magazine*, December 2000).

CHAPTER 43

You Are the Keeper of the HR Ethics

● ●

With the seemingly endless list of corporate scandals that are plaguing our times, as a nation we're now asking ourselves what we can learn from the unfolding misadventures of corporate America: What protections we can install inside corporate law, what preventions we can install inside corporate management, and how individual Americans can avoid losing so much personal wealth in the future. The damage that hard-working employees have suffered is almost beyond measure, and I predict that the national accounting for the losses has only just begun. And perhaps it is this impact that has finally dragged HR into the national debate on such a large scale.

The extraordinarily personal impact of this current corporate corruption story on employees has had the effect of laying much of the responsibility directly at HR's feet. In fact, not long after the breaking of the Enron story (with all those shattered 401(k) accounts), a few self-styled HR thought leaders and provocateurs started asking, "Where was HR in all of this?"

The answer to that particular question will come out as all the corruption cases are investigated over the next few years. What's more to the point is the question that will help us move forward, wiser for having watched the unfolding business sagas of our times. And that question is: What is HR's *power* to promote the ethical spirit of each corporation? I predict that if we don't address this question very carefully, the very word *ethics* will eventually take on the shopworn tedium of all the other words that once were our favorite, bright, and shiny concepts: *reengineering*, *right-sizing*, *open-book*, *empowered*, *TQM*, and so on. HR's power in the corporate ethics conversation lies in keeping the expectation and standards of ethics alive inside our company, refreshed every day with every hard decision that forces us to choose between the expedient and the morally correct. If we don't want the ethics discussion to be merely the flavor of the month, we have to make sure that we address HR's role in corporate ethics with courage and candor.

To respond directly to the question of where HR was in the corporate scandals that are currently before us, I'd first like to say that by the time the ripple effects of those corporate decisions had finally reached the HR department, the head of HR had already lost any arguments he or she might have been able to put forward. The wink-wink, nod-nod way of doing business was already so endemic in the corporate biosphere that there was nothing HR could have done to protect either the business, the shareholders, or the employees from the infection.

To imply that HR is the corporate conscience—its ethical shepherd—is absurd and counterproductive. When companies are truly ethical, that burden is shared by everyone throughout the company, from top management on down. Everyone has the responsibility to make decisions based on the values espoused by both the company and the person's own conscience—and it's not too idealistic to expect those value sets to be consistent, if not one and the same. In an environment in which integrity is part of the very air that people breathe, it's rare that any one person is faced with the difficult choice between his or her self-respect and the corporate interest.

In a genuinely ethical corporate environment, the HR leader is not a stern, desiccated schoolmarm wagging her finger and reciting a litany of "thou shalt nots." If you find yourself in that role, my advice to you is to find a new job and be quick about it. For as long as you are associated with that company, you will not be able to use the HR function as a tool for growth (for either the enterprise or yourself). You will be the resident killjoy, the "downer," the wet blanket on tantalizing, but illegal, schemes. And, unless you happen to like testifying in a court of law or before Congress, there's not much of an upside to your association with such an operation. Ultimately, if yours is the lone voice of morality in a culture that easily overlooks questions of what is right, you'll soon be ejected from the group anyway.

Even in the most ethical companies, you may find yourself facing challenges to your commitment to do the right thing. Don't be too quick to judge. These challenges may not reflect an environmental ethical disconnect as much as they reflect a lack of understanding of HR and the laws you must follow. Remember, you're the HR expert, and you know better than anyone else how sacrosanct HR laws and practices are. It's up to you to establish standards and expectations to uphold those laws. And you can do so while still serving your client's interests.

I had a boss once who casually said to me, "Why do you need to spend all this money printing summary plan descriptions for the benefits plan? That's a huge expense, so let's not do it anymore." I explained to her that the Employment Retirement Income Security Act (ERISA) actually requires us to publish this information. Her response was, "Well, they probably wouldn't catch it. Our employees don't think it's valuable, and it's such a big expense. So let's just skip it, shall we?"

No, we shall not. Breaking the law is one of my personal nonnegotiables. I'm funny that way. But I knew fundamentally that her driving interest was saving money, not the legal aspects of ERISA. She had the financial interests of the business at heart, and she was right that the employees probably couldn't care less. But the law is the law. And so I found ways to reduce the costs of printing the information (serving her real need), all the while staying on the right side of the law (doing the right thing—and protecting both myself and my company's interests).

Although standing up for what is ethical may be a daily responsibility for everyone (not just HR), one of these days you may encounter an intransigent boss who presents you with an impossible (and illegal) demand. The request is clearly out of your value bounds. You won't even consider it. The trouble is, you know that the request won't stop with you. Your boss will find someone else to do the dirty work, and once it's done, it will have devastating effects on the company, its reputation, its market value, and its employees. What do you do?

Don't take it outside. Take it to the top. Go over your boss's head. If that doesn't work, go over that boss's head. If that doesn't work, keep climbing the organizational ladder until you reach the CEO, if you have to. Now that new laws are making CEOs personally accountable for their companies' actions, you may find a more receptive ear than you might have found even a year ago. In most cases, you won't have to go any further. But if you are still not heard, your next option is simple: Go to the board. By this time your job is in jeopardy anyway, so you have nothing to lose (except your self-respect or perhaps your freedom if the request is illegal and you comply with it).

Blow the whistle publicly only as an absolute last resort. The negative publicity can damage the company irreparably, throwing your coworkers out of their jobs and destroying the company's stock value. By giving the company every opportunity to fix the problem internally, you will have served everyone's interests, kept people's livelihoods intact, and improved a corporate situation immeasurably.

Business history is full of difficult choices where several "right things to do" are in conflict. But it both saddens and gladdens me that the business community has been forced to return to the fundamentals of right and wrong. It saddens me because so many of these issues are self-evident and basic, and I am appalled that we have to return to them as a refresher course under duress. But I'm also gladdened because I, like so many other business observers over the recent years, have been marveling at how the marketplace no longer rewards long-term-oriented decision making. It seems to be interested only in short-term returns. The prevailing attitude, especially in the late 1990s, is that if you're not making a quick profit, you're going to fail. It's not hard to understand how the sparkling promise of definite higher returns can push the philosophical argument about right and wrong into the murky shadows. Now there's a nationwide outcry for truth, corporate responsibility, and business morality. And it's been a long time coming.

And now when HR agitators start squawking, "Where was HR when all this was going down?" I hope that we'll all be able to say proudly, "Minding our own business"—the business of growing companies that are both ethically grounded and immensely successful in the marketplace.

Integrity: The New Competitive Edge for Recruiting Talent?

Job seekers are discovering that having certain employers on their résumé just might be a liability. Having worked at the companies that were in the headlines in 2002, for example, may prove to be an embarrassment. Can individuals separate their own personal reputations from the besmirched reputation of their employer? I can only hope that hiring managers around the world know the difference between a personal performance record and organizational behavior.

Still, as hiring managers seek to recruit top talent, they may find themselves selling their companies on the strength of their values statement. According to "Wanted: Ethical Employer" (*Wall Street Journal*, July 9, 2002), there may be a growing pressure for hiring managers not only to sell the value of the opportunity they're offering candidates, but also to promote their values statement and moral track record. In the article, Linda K. Trevino, chair of the Department of Management and Organization, Smeal College of Business, Pennsylvania State University, advises job seekers to conduct an "ethics audit" of the company, making sure that key evidence of a lively values culture is in place. Among the things to look for are:

- A formal ethics code that is widely distributed

- Training in ethical decision-making techniques that is made available throughout the ranks

- The availability of formal reporting channels

- Swift and just discipline for unethical conduct

- A cultural emphasis on integrity and ethical behavior, both for new employees and throughout the company

Be careful how you promote your company as an honest business. There's a fine line between being earnest and being in poor taste. I'm sure you have one or two businesses in your community that make a *really* big point of their honesty: A pawnshop, maybe? A mechanic? An attorney? You know the kind I mean: The more they emphasize their honesty, the more you're tempted to think, "Maybe not so much."

The record—or lack thereof—should speak for itself.

CHAPTER 44

Conclusion
How Do We Get There From Here?

What I've shown you throughout this book is a new landscape for human resources. New possibilities. New elevations. New ways of navigating. New ways of understanding what we're seeing. New landmarks. New destinations.

And I hope I've given you a glimpse of the best destination of all: a powerful, positive career with a first-class, people-oriented organization whose mission is to improve the lives of its customers—*all* its customers—around the world. That destination is within the reach of all of us, no matter who we are, where we live, or the nature of our company. You just need to know how to get there.

"How do we get there from here?" That has been a basic navigation question that mankind has asked since the Stone Age. At Southwest, I learned that pilots ask and answer that question by filing flight plans. So, in that special spirit of customer service, I am concluding this book with a flight plan for you to follow as you build your own from-the-heart career in HR. These are the major points you must cover in order to reach your destination:

■ *Choose organizations that value their people and their people department.* These don't have to be completely evolved companies (in fact, half the fun could be in helping them achieve their people goals). But the senior leadership must be sincere in its objective of manifesting its vision of the future through the power and passion of its employees.

■ *Keep in mind that it's all about business first.* Where many well-intentioned HR professionals go wrong is by failing to recognize and respond to the business needs first. You have to be able to make tough decisions, but you can make the tough decisions from the heart.

■ *Remember that it's personal for your people.* Have a genuine affection for and connection to your coworkers. Never forget that every decision you make in HR has a direct impact on their personal lives. No matter who they are or what they do in your company, work is part of their life story. It's where they spend so many hours of their day.

■ *Build trust by being consistent with your stated values.* In a trust-based organization, everyone can concentrate on the work and the future, confident that the *right* thing is being done and the *right* choice is being made at every given moment.

■ *Cultivate an innovative, solutions-oriented environment that doesn't punish risk taking.* People need to be able to take risks, especially in today's marketplace, which demands new, different, never-seen-before products day in and day out. Not every attempt or idea is going to work out brilliantly. Reassure people that they can afford to make a few mistakes.

■ *Make your employees Customer Number One.* Build your business to be a deeply rewarding customer service organization that gives your employees the chance to experience firsthand what great customer service feels like. When their relationship with your company is of high quality and is built on trust, respect, and service, they will treat your external customers with the same care and attention to detail.

■ *Use all the resources that are available to you to grow in both your career and your job.* We have never had so many opportunities to learn and grow as we do today: The Internet, professional associates and colleagues, research, associations, and formal education programs designed specifically to prepare students for a lifelong career in HR as strategic business partners.

■ *Make your organization's agenda your agenda.* Even though business priorities and people policies may conflict now and then, overall they should be one and the same. One of your most important roles is to be an advocate for the employees, but you should never be antagonistic to other business interests and concerns. Senior leaders and employees alike should always regard your department as the source of both the best pro-business outcomes and the best pro-people outcomes.

■ *Remember that you are neither saint nor savior.* The personal lives of hundreds, if not thousands, of people may rest on your shoulders, directly affected by every single decision you make or program you create. You are the keeper of personal confidences. You are the custodian of corporate strategies. There are many times when you must rise above your own personal preferences and emotions for the sake of the greater good. And you must look at yourself in the mirror every day. You will be called upon to deny your own personal preferences, wishes, and ambitions for the sake of the greater good. But don't make a habit of denying your own personal needs or your most dearly held objectives and goals. If you regularly subjugate your own priorities, you will be no good for anyone. Above all, stay true to your ethics, even if it means that your job is on the line. You will have to answer to someone. It's far better that it be the face in the mirror than a Senate investigative committee.

It's a widely accepted fact that HR has been on the receiving end of a great deal of disrespect and second-guessing over the years. As a result, we've been living with a community inferiority complex that has been dragging us down and keeping us from leading and creating amazing change inside our companies. We want to be actively involved in helping our companies shape their future and their strategy. And we want to be recognized for the value that we bring to our organizations.

We can achieve those gains and those goals if we use our heads and remember to use our hearts.

That's what it takes to build a great business.

Recommended Reading List

The 100 Best Companies to Work For in America. Robert Levering and Milton Moskowitz. New York: Doubleday Currency, 1993.

1001 Ways to Reward Employees. Bob Nelson. New York: Workman Publishing, 1994.

Assimilating New Leaders: The Key to Executive Retention. Diane Downey and Tom March. New York: AMACOM, 2001.

The Bible, any edition.

Bodacious! An AOL Insider Cracks the Code to Outrageous Success for Women. Mary E. Foley with Martha I. Finney. New York: AMACOM, 2001.

Built to Last: Successful Habits of Visionary Companies. James C. Collins and Jerry I. Porras. New York: HarperBusiness, 1994.

Certification Guide: The Professional Edge for Your Career. Raymond B. Weinberg. Alexandria, VA: Society for Human Resource Management, 2002.

Contented Cows Give Better Milk: The Plain Truth About Employee Relations and Your Bottom Line. Bill Catlette and Richard Hadden. Germantown, TN: Saltillo Press, 2000.

Corporate Culture and Performance. John P. Kotter with James L. Heskett. New York: Simon and Schuster, 1992.

Creating a Total Rewards Strategy: A Toolkit for Designing Business-Based Plans. Todd M. Manas and Michael Dennis Graham. New York: AMACOM, 2003.

Customer Service: Extraordinary Results at Southwest Airlines, Charles Schwab, Lands' End, American Express, Staples, and USAA. Fred Wierseman (ed.). New York: HarperBusiness, 1998.

Delivering Results: A New Mandate for Human Resource Professionals. Dave Ulrich (ed.). Boston: Harvard Business School Publishing, 1998.

Discipline of Market Leaders: Choose Your Customers, Narrow Your Focus, Dominate Your Market. Michael Treacy and Fred Wiersma. Reading, Mass.: Addison-Wesley, 1995.

Find Your Calling, Love Your Life. Martha Finney and Deborah Dasch. New York: Simon and Schuster, 1998.

Fun Works: Creating Places Where People Love to Work. Leslie Yerkes. San Francisco: Berrett-Koehler Publishers, Inc., 2001.

Generations at Work: Managing the Clash of Veterans, Boomers, Xers, and Nexters in Your Workplace. Ron Zemke, Claire Raines, and Bob Filipczak. New York: AMACOM, 2000.

Get Weird! 101 Innovative Ways to Make Your Company a Great Place to Work. John Putzier. New York: AMACOM, 2001.

Getting Employees to Fall in Love with Your Company. Jim Harris. New York: AMACOM, 1996.

Good Company: Caring as Fiercely as You Compete. Hal Rosenbluth and Diane McFerrin Peters. Reading, Mass.: Addison-Wesley, 1998.

Handle with CARE: Motivating and Retaining Your Employees. Barbara A. Glanz. New York: McGraw-Hill, 2002.

Hidden Value: How Great Companies Achieve Extraordinary Results with Ordinary People. Charles A. O'Reilly and Jeffrey Pfeffer. Boston: Harvard Business School Publishing, 2000.

High Performance HR: Leveraging Human Resources for the Competitive Advantage. David S. Weiss. Toronto: John Wiley & Sons, 1999, 2000.

The HR Scorecard: Linking People, Strategy, and Performance. Mark A. Huselid, David Ulrick, and Brian Becker. Boston: Harvard Business School Publishing, 2001.

The Human Capital Edge: 21 People Management Practices Your Company Must Implement (or Avoid) to Maximize Shareholder Value. Bruce N. Pfau and Ira T. Kay. New York: McGraw-Hill, 2001.

Human Resource Champions. David Ulrich. Boston: Harvard Business School Press, 1996.

Intangibles: Management, Measurement, and Reporting. Baruch Lev. Washington, D.C.: The Brookings Institution Press, 2001.

The Leadership Engine: How Winning Companies Build Leaders at Every Level. Noel M. Tichy with Eli Cohen. New York: Harper-Business, 1997.

Liberating the Corporate Soul: Building a Visionary Organization. Richard Barrett. Boston: Butterworth Heinemann, 1998.

Love 'Em or Lose 'Em: Getting Good People to Stay, 2nd ed. Beverly Kay and Sharon Jordan-Evans. San Francisco: Berrett-Koehler Publishers, 2002.

Love Is the Killer App: How to Win Business and Influence Friends. Tim Sanders. New York: Crown Business, 2002.

Loyalty Rules! How Today's Leaders Build Lasting Relationships. Frederick F. Reichheld. Boston: Harvard Business School Publishing, 2001.

Making Mergers Work: The Strategic Importance of People. Jeffrey A. Schmidt (ed.). A Towers Perrin/SHRM Foundation Publication, October, 2001.

Man's Search for Meaning. Viktor Frankl. New York: Washington Square Press, 1997.

96 Great Interview Questions to Ask Before You Hire. Paul Falcone. New York: AMACOM, 1996.

Recommended Reading List

Nuts! Southwest Airlines' Crazy Recipes for Business and Personal Success. Kevin Freiberg and Jackie Freiberg. New York: Bantam Doubleday Dell, 1998.

Peak Performance: Aligning the Hearts and Minds of Your Employees. Jon R. Katzenbach. Boston: Harvard Business School Publishing, 2000.

Positively Outrageous Service: How to Delight and Astound Your Customers and Win Them for Life. T. Scott Gross. New York: Warner Books, 1994.

The Power of a Good Fight. Lynne Eisaguirre. Indianapolis: Alpha Books, 2002.

The Reward Plan Advantage: A Manager's Guide to Improving Business Performance Through People. Jerry L. McAdams. San Francisco: Jossey-Bass, 1996.

The ROI of Human Capital. Jac Fitz-enz. New York: AMACOM, 2000.

Simplicity: The New Competitive Advantage in a World of More, Better, Faster. Bill Jensen. Cambridge, MA: Perseus Publishing, 2001.

Strategic Human Resource Leader: How to Prepare Your Organization for Six Key Trends Shaping the Future. William J, Rothwell, Robert K. Prescott, and Maria W. Taylor. Palo Alto, Calif.: Davies-Black Publishing, 1998.

The Turbo Charged Company, Igniting Your Business to Soar Ahead of the Competition. Larry Goddard and David Brown. York Publishing Co., 1995.

Voices of Diversity: Real People Talk About Problems and Solutions in a Workplace Where Everyone Is Not Alike. Renee Blank and Sandra Slipp. New York: AMACOM, 1994.

The War for Talent. Ed Michaels, Beth Axelrod, and Helen Handfield-Jones. Boston: Harvard Business School Publishing, 2001.

Weird Ideas That Work, 11½ Practices for Promoting, Managing and Sustaining Innovation. Robert I. Sutton. New York: Free Press, 2002.

What Every Successful Woman Knows. Janice Reals Ellig and William J. Morin. New York: McGraw-Hill, 2001.

What the CEO Wants You to Know: How Your Company Really Works. Ram Charan. New York: Crown, 2001.

The Working Life: The Promise and Betrayal of Modern Work. Joanne B. Ciulla. New York: Time Books, Random House, 2000.

Index

Index

Index

Index

About the Authors

Libby Sartain, SPHR, CCP (Woodside, CA), SVP Human Resources and Chief People Yahoo, Yahoo! Inc. is responsible for leading Yahoo! Inc.'s global human resources strategy and leading and developing the human resources team. This team focuses on attracting, retaining, and developing Yahoo!'s employees who promote and strengthen the company culture, as well as represent the powerful Yahoo! brand. Prior to joining Yahoo!, Sartain was "vice president people" at Southwest Airlines Co., where she led all human resources functions, including employment, learning and development, benefits, and compensation. She also played a key role in developing an employment brand strategy which helped double employee growth during her tenure as HR Chief. Sartain served as chairman of the Society for Human Resource Management in 2001 and was named fellow of the National Academy of Human Resources. She can be contacted at libby@hrfromtheheart.com.

Martha I. Finney (Los Gatos, CA) is a veteran business journalist and consultant specializing in leadership communication, HR, and employee engagement. She is also the author, co-author or ghostwriter of eight books. She can be reached at Martha@marthafinney.com.